Pioneers Scholars & Rogues

Pioneers, Scholars & Rogues

A Spirited History of the University of Oregon

Eugene, Oregon

Copyright © 2002 University of Oregon Press
All rights reserved. No part of this book may be reproduced in any form without written permission from the publisher.

Published by
University of Oregon Press
5283 University of Oregon
Eugene, OR 97403-5283

Designed and edited by Jeffrey Jane Flowers with additional editorial assistance from Jessica MacMurray and Tom Hager.

COVER IMAGES
Front cover: Dads' Gates at Homecoming circa 1945, University Day 1919, Luella Clay Carson, Slow Race on Hayward Field 1914; all from the University of Oregon Special Collections and Archives.
Back cover: Picnics 1890 and 1980, Women and WAAC poster 1945; from the University of Oregon Special Collections and Archives.
Mascot photograph by Jack Liu.

Book manufactured in the United States

ISBN: 0-87114-300-3

h g f e d c b a

Contents

1876-1900
THE SCHOOL ON THE HILL 3
Milestones 14
Presidents: John Wesley Johnson 5 ❖ Charles Hiram Chapman 11
Profiles: Matthew P. Deady 4 ❖ Henry Villard 8 ❖ Samson H. Friendly 15
  ❖ Luella Clay Carson 16 ❖ Thomas Condon 21
Features: Early Sports 18

1900-1929
THE ROWDY RAGTIME YEARS 23
Milestones 42
Presidents: Frank Strong 27 ❖ Prince Lucien Campbell 31
Profiles: Bill Hayward 28 ❖ Irene Gerlinger 30 ❖ Ellis Lawrence 37
  ❖ James Gilbert 41
Features: Sports 33 ❖ McArthur Court 39 ❖ Pioneer Father 40

1929-1950
DEPRESSION, WAR AND RENAISSANCE 45
Milestones 60
Presidents: Arnold Bennett Hall 47 ❖ Clarence Valentine Boyer 51
  ❖ Donald Milton Erb 54 ❖ Harry K. Newburn 59
Profiles: Eric Allen 49
Features: Sports 52 ❖ Oregon Goes to War 56 ❖ Pioneer Mother 58
  ❖ Library History 61

1951-1975
SWEETHEARTS AND SIT-INS 63
Milestones 70
Presidents: O. Meredith Wilson 67 ❖ Arthur S. Flemming 74
  ❖ Robert D. Clark 81
Profiles: Bill Bowerman 68 ❖ Ralph Huestis 73 ❖ Orlando John Hollis 75
  ❖ Golda Wickham 77
Features: How to Get into College 65 ❖ Track Town USA 79

1976-2001
CREATING A NEW UNIVERSITY 83
Milestones 98
Presidents: William Beaty Boyd 85 ❖ Paul Olum 88
  ❖ Myles Brand 91 ❖ Dave Frohnmayer 95
Profiles: Bill Loy 87 ❖ George Streisinger 92 ❖ Joan Acker 96
Features: Science Complex 93 ❖ Oregon Campaign 99

NOTABLE DUCKS: FAMOUS ALUMNI 100
MORE FACTS & FIGURES 105
INDEX 106
SOURCES AND ACKNOWLEDGEMENTS 108

Graduating class, 1879.

Deady Hall and classroom (inset) on opening day, 1876.

John Straub, professor of Greek, hired in 1882 and in active service at the UO until 1930.

THE School ON THE Hill

by Walter Wentz

Dear Brother Tom:
    I have now been here some three weeks. I am very well pleased with the town and with the people. Eugene is a pretty place and surrounded by beautiful hills over which the Eugene people dote very much... .

So wrote George Shinn to his brother Thomas, of Union, Oregon. The year was 1883, and George was a new student at the young "Oregon State University" at Eugene.

The pretty little town of Eugene City was a place of dust in summer, mud in winter; of narrow board sidewalks and a few scattered lampposts bearing kerosene streetlights flanking dirt streets; of gracious, white-painted houses with the family cow, as like as not, quartered in the back yard.

Eugene was a staid and Godfearing place, saturated with the Protestant work ethic. It had as many saloons as churches, but into those saloons young George Shinn was forbidden to go.

He had voluntarily entered a small, exclusive and strangely cloistered group, the University students of Eugene. His days were spent in recitation before classmates.

So it had been since 1876, when the first tiny class assembled at the University, a fine brick building standing on a bare and muddy knoll a bit east of Eugene proper. New students were welcomed in the assembly room in an informal occasion called the "walk-around," in which they met their classmates and professors. After that they were on their own.

They had to find their own lodging, choosing from "The Castle" of Mrs. Underwood, down by the depot, or Croner's or Grandma Fitch's, near 10th and Willamette, or some chilly attic

Before 1900, the University had "the atmosphere of a petty theological seminary manned by superannuated ministers." The academic program was brutal, and the "Ten Commandments" ruled out dating, tobacco, alcohol, dancing and boxing.

room, depending on how much they could afford. And many couldn't afford much, having to "bach it" in the most hungry and uncomfortable situations.

They had to order their books from downtown shops, well in advance of classes.

They had to study diligently to keep in perfect form for recitations, orations and essays in class; and always they had to live, talk and act discreetly, knowing that the town was small and that censorious eyes observed their behavior.

So it was with George Shinn, in the year 1883. His life in Eugene City was regulated by a set of "Rules for the Government of Students..." called the "Ten Commandments," drawn up by the University's patriarchal president, John Wesley Johnson:

* A student could not enter a saloon, under pain of expulsion.
* Nor could one drink any alcoholic beverage while attending the University, or while traveling to or from it—despite the fact that many young frontiersmen were in their twenties before they could afford to pay the University tuition.
* Nor could one use tobacco in any form.
* Nor could one be outside one's room past 11:00 P.M.

And so on, for six more Commandments.

MATTHEW P. DEADY: PIONEERING SUPPORTER

Oregon's first and only federal judge for thirty-four years, Matthew P. Deady was among the earliest and most influential friends of the University. He drafted and lobbied for its 1876 legislative charter, became its first Board of Regents president, appointed its first faculty and helped save it from an early bankruptcy. A grateful University named its first building Deady Hall, which became a National Historic Landmark in 1978.

Born in Maryland and a blacksmith apprentice at age sixteen, Deady earned a teaching certificate and moved west in 1849. Dazzled by the beauty of Mt. Hood as he canoed down the Columbia, he settled first in Oregon City.

In 1853, U.S. President Franklin Pierce appointed Deady to the Territorial Supreme Court, a position he held until statehood in 1859. At that time, he accepted appointment as Oregon's first federal district judge, which he remained until his death.

As president of the 1857 constitutional convention, he helped to create much of the fundamental law that still governs Oregonians today. He wrote the state's first codes of civil and criminal procedure, its first penal code, a landmark corporations statute and many more specialized laws. During his thirty-four years on the federal bench, Deady wrote hundreds of opinions on topics as diverse as admiralty law, bankruptcy, immigration, constitutional law, criminal law and public land law.

However, none of Matthew Deady's service to his state and nation has endured longer or more profitably for more Oregonians than his early contributions to the University. His legislative charter secured for the school both an improved initial funding base and the fundamental principle of academic freedom that "no sectarian or political test shall ever be applied" to any University appointment. In 1876, Judge Deady selected the University's motto, *Mens Agitat Molem*.

—Ralph James Mooney

John Wesley Johnson
President 1876–1893

In 1876, John Wesley Johnson, president and professor of Latin, registered the first official student body at the institution that would become the University of Oregon. It was a momentous event for UO—and hard won for a motivated, committed educator.

Johnson was fourteen when his father sold the family farm in Missouri and moved to Oregon. His mother and sister died of cholera en route and were buried in unmarked graves along the Oregon Trail. The family settled in Benton County.

Although the young Johnson was eager to read and learn from books, he did not learn the alphabet until after the age of ten. Opportunities for higher education were limited in Corvallis, so in 1854 he enrolled at Pacific University in Forest Grove where he had Thomas Condon for a teacher. This whetted his appetite for more education, and he and a cousin set out for New Haven, Connecticut, via San Francisco, Panama and New York. After walking from New York City to New Haven, Johnson presented himself for admission to Yale. Though he lacked the necessary background, the faculty allowed him to enter conditionally.

He graduated in 1862, sixth in a class of 100. The years at Yale molded him into a classical scholar; but they left him ill from poor diet and hard study, and with a debt of $2,000 borrowed from a brother-in-law at 12 percent interest. His health kept him out of the Union Army, so he returned to Oregon. Having taught school briefly before going east, he decided to try it again. He joined the faculty at the Methodist College in Corvallis, but his health forced him to seek out-of-doors employment. After a time in the Idaho mining camps, his health improved and he returned to Oregon to accept a position as principal of McMinnville College (now Linfield).

After four years, he became principal of a grammar department of a Portland school. Two years later he was instrumental in establishing the first high school in the Pacific Northwest, now Lincoln High School, and served as principal for ten years.

In 1876 he came to Eugene and was selected by the Board of Regents to become the first president and faculty member of the new University. The new job required dedication and Johnson responded. His classes were textbook-based and he maintained strict discipline. He was unusually successful in "imparting the beauty of the flexible and sonorous Greek and the robust and vigorous construction of the Latin," wrote student B.B. Beekman.

President Johnson's duties included those of registrar, business officer, provost, dean of students and secretary. He was against social dancing and even roller skating as a pastime.

Yet, considering the time and facilities at hand, Johnson served the University well through its crucial early years. He understood the people of Oregon and their suspicion of higher education. Time and time again, he urged the regents to expand the curriculum, to establish departments and to organize the University in the style of Yale or the University of California at Berkeley.

Law, medicine and art were added during Johnson's tenure but not the departments of engineering and mines that he so badly wanted. The board ignored his requests for reorganization and the idea of departments was deferred. Granting a degree without a language was allowed over his protest and that of the faculty.

During the seventeen years of Johnson's presidency, quality of education, not quantity, essentials rather than diversities, and thoroughness rather than versatility were the rule.

During the seventeen years of Johnson's presidency, quality of education, not quantity, essentials rather than diversities and thoroughness rather than versatility were the rule. He was a generous man, wholly honest, fair with his associates and students. Although his health was always poor, he never missed a class in more than twenty years.

—Keith Richard

The School on the Hill

Of course some students were restive under the Ten Commandments, and, in classic student fashion, this opposition took the form of satire. One month after the president's rules were published in 1882, the students published "Commandments Promulgated to the Disciples..." which recast Johnson's rules in biblical form. Johnson himself was referred to as "the Father":

III. Neither shall thou use Tobacco, after the manner of the Father. (Johnson smoked like a furnace.)

But student protest had to remain anonymous, for the eight old-school autocrats of the faculty brooked no open opposition. All of them had religious backgrounds, and several were ordained ministers. The old minutes of faculty meetings are full of disciplinary notes, items concerning students expelled for drunkenness, or even for being seen going into any of Eugene's many saloons; a young couple informed that they would have to stop keeping company or both leave the University; a young man who was requested not to re-enter the University because the faculty had heard something which seemed to indicate "he was not such as to his character as he ought to be."

Some recourse was possible. Accused students might go before a faculty meeting to defend themselves. Or, if their offense was judged venial, they might only be required to make public apology before the faculty or the assembled student body, which must have been a nightmare of humiliation in those days.

Were those faculty members complete ogres? Hardly. Their ferocious morality was apparently typical of the time and place. In George Shinn's old letter, we have a sympathetic if somewhat sentimental portrait of these old-school tyrants:

> I have entered school and like the teachers. I went in to the President's room yesterday morning to pay my tuition while the class was reciting in Sallust. I was afraid to go in at first, as I had heard the Prof. was very cross; but after I sat awhile and listened to the recitation I thought surely that he had been misrepresented to me; for one of the students got his translation mixed up & finally failed outright. The Prof. talked very kind to him, and encouraged him so much like a loving father, that one of the girls who had lately arrived, wept....
>
> Pretty soon another student failed on pronouncing a word. The Prof. then told the class a very funny story about "Tecumseh" which made us all laugh till our sides were sore....
>
> ...I went into Prof. Bailey's room to recite Geometry. Business is business in there I tell you.... He sometimes grows enthusiastic

---

The aim of a college is to cultivate the mind in a general way by disciplining all the faculties, to make the young strong in intellect, to give them acute, polished, well-balanced minds. If this disciplinary work is well-accomplished, the mind may afterwards be applied to any subject, to the study of any profession, art, or business and it will be able to work with precision, ease and power.
—From a UO catalog, 1885

1876–1900

The University's Observatory on Skinner Butte encouraged studies of the stars and planets from 1877–1895. The building's foundation still exists as part of the reservoir constructed in the 1950s.

Major Facilities and Additions * 1876–1900	
Name	Year
Deady Hall	1876
Villard Hall	1886
Friendly Hall	1893

*10,000 square feet or more

Memorial Day celebration at Villard Hall, circa 1893.

like the famous Knight of La Mancha and imagines that this is West Point, that we are cadets & that he is the Professor of mathematics in that National institution....

I next recited to Prof. Burke in Rhetoric. He is the youngest teacher in the institution, and is not married. They say he used to be a great favorite among the ladies. But he is now the homeliest man in town and is going into a confirmed bachelorhood. He loves solitude like an owl, and you can often see him walking toward the graveyard in the deepening twilight of evening.... Not withstanding his pensiveness, he is an excellent teacher and is well liked thro' out the school.

The social life of George Shinn and his classmates was not, of course, completely sterile. Students were forbidden to attend dances, or the theater or even to hear church-sponsored lectures without the permission of the all-powerful faculty. But there were other things—among them the student literary societies.

There were two of these, the Laurean for the men and the Eutaxian for the women. The University long resisted the introduction of fraternities and sororities popular in the East—in fact, there was a Commandment against joining any "secret college society." But the old-fashioned debating societies filled a definite social need, and they were founded as a matter of course when

HENRY VILLARD: BENEFACTOR IN A CRISIS

In 1881, the University needed a savior. Old debts, contracted years earlier and totaling $7,830.91, came like a ghost from the past to precipitate a new crisis. By July, various creditors secured judgments against the property of the University and placed writs of execution in the hands of the sheriff. The fate of the University was gloomy.

Meanwhile, the news of the impending sale of the University building appeared in the Portland newspaper and caught the eye of Henry Villard, the foremost financial leader and railroad promoter in the Northwest. Always a man of keen intellectual interests, Villard believed in developing the educational as well as the economic resources of the developing western country.

He wrote to Judge Deady, president of the Board of Regents, expressing a willingness to assume responsibility for the debt. Additional interest and legal fees brought the debt total to $8,181.89. Villard paid $7,000 and the Eugene citizens' committee covered the remainder. Late in October, Mr. Villard visited the University and was given a rousing reception.

Not content with simply meeting the emergency, Villard looked into the condition of the University and noted the absence of certain necessary tools of instruction. Additional gifts were made for library books, physical and chemical apparatus and $250 scholarships to be offered to the five most meritorious students of the year. He paid the salary for the professor of English literature from appointment to November, 1882. A year later, these gifts were consolidated into a present of $50,000 in bonds of the Northern Pacific Railroad. Mr. Villard's generosity attracted wide attention, as his donations were the first of any importance to public education in Oregon.

—*Henry D. Sheldon*

Senior Class Picnic, 1890.

the first students entered the newborn University in the autumn of 1876.

These societies met once a week: it was an eagerly contested distinction to be elected an officer of one. They held lengthy debates on such earth-shaking topics as "Does the present aspect of things portend the fall of the American Republic?" or "Resolved, that dancing is a pleasant and harmless amusement." Whether the affirmative or the negative viewpoint won the debate was not so important as the high-flung oratory and flowering rhetoric in which the contending speakers expressed themselves.

About 40 percent of the University men belonged to the Laureans, and about 20 percent of the women to the Eutaxians, but their meetings were open to all, providing harmless amusement for those who had time to attend. A room was assigned for their meetings, and the societies accumulated the first University library. George Shinn continues in his letter to brother Thomas:

> I visited the Laurean Literary Society last night. I wish you could have been with us. The Laureans have a nice hall very well furnished. They do good work when they have plenty of money in their treasury & enjoy themselves in real luxurious style. They sometimes make handsome appropriations for evening refreshments & then those who are away on that evening & do not get any of the

> The university served a distinct place in the community life. The annual commencement, a dignified occasion where one might hear each graduate deliver one of those rhetorical and idealistic orations so dear to the heart of the Anglo-Saxon, supplied the need of a spectacle in a community where such occasions were infrequent. The citizens of Eugene attended and farmers of the adjacent region came in such large numbers that long lines of waiting wagons would be seen in the neighborhood of the campus.
> —Henry D. Sheldon

The School on the Hill

THE CONDON OAKS

When the University opened in 1876, the only trees on campus were two white oaks, above, standing just northeast of Villard Hall. Today, the gracefully pruned giants are encrusted with moss, ferns and mistletoe. The trees, which are more than 300 years old, are known as the Condon Oaks.

good things, look down their noses & talk naughty about their brothers. The two societies have a very fine library numbering about 1100 volumes.

Of course, the godlike faculty could not completely control the students' private lives, and the decorous romances of that era could go on in the private homes or boarding houses of Eugene, with the proper chaperones, of course. Shinn describes the rules of etiquette, an odd blend of tact and practicality:

First, when you want to take a drive, go in with some other fellow & hire a buggy. Then engage your girl; if your girl cannot go, do not ask another, that would be making her second choice, but get some other fellow to persuade his sister to go along. She will do just as well, and you will never know the difference a hundred years from now....

Athletics drained off some of the bottled-up energy of students. Baseball clubs were organized as early as 1877, but calamitous defeats kept them from becoming permanent. In 1883,

UO Baseball, 1893–4.

Charles Hiram Chapman
President 1893–1899

At the age of thirty-two, Charles Hiram Chapman had a Ph.D. in mathematics and a brilliant academic and teaching record at Johns Hopkins. When he took the reins of the presidency at Oregon, Chapman found a divided faculty. He was polite to both sides and advised them that they were to teach—not fight—and that the University suffered from bickering.

Chapman's solution was to involve himself in every level of decision-making. He proposed to the physics and mathematics teachers that they should have laboratories, and teach accordingly. Chapman made himself chairman of every faculty committee to make certain his mandates were obeyed. While this was effective, it led to an exceedingly centralized administration.

But Chapman was able to make wholesale changes in curriculum. He added biology; civil, mining and electrical engineering; business classes; physical training and—the greatest horror at the time—the elective system.

Opposition to Chapman grew in Eugene. Unable to fault his educational goals, the leaders of the community attacked him personally. He did not pay enough property tax, he believed in evolution, he bought his groceries in Portland, his wife practiced medicine and was a suffragette, he had been cited for riding his horse too fast in the city.

Chapman's bathtub was a symbol of his problems. When the Regents purchased George Collier's house on 13th Avenue, they proposed to move the president into the second floor if he would agree to pay rent and have the remodeling done at his expense. He agreed, and had a bathtub installed as part of the remodeling. Believing that the tub was a permanent improvement, Chapman asked the Regents to pay for it. The local paper attacked both this spendthrift notion and the idea of bathtubs generally. Chapman paid for the tub and the installation. When he resigned, the tub went with him.

Eventually, petitions were presented to the Regents for the removal of Chapman and certain faculty members. After holding discussions for several days with students, faculty and others, the Board voted unanimously to ignore the petitions.

Chapman liberalized the curriculum, brought in the "elective" class idea, and taught his own classes by the lecture system, assigning a stunning workload of outside reading.

Chapman had gained a wide following among citizens of the state. This led to respect for the University in intellectual circles. He traveled around the state to give extension lectures, holding a series in Portland and Salem. He began summer institutes for teachers to upgrade education in the common schools. The better scholars at the University praised Chapman, and a legislative committee appointed to investigate the University reported back to Salem with high praise for Chapman, the faculty, students and the University.

Salaries were sometimes cut to meet the budget, to hire additional faculty or to finance needed equipment for labs or classrooms. Chapman was able to convince the Board that this was necessary—but it did not endear him to the faculty.

After the June board meeting in 1898, in which petitions for his dismissal were presented, Chapman thought it best to resign. He felt that the enemies he had made would continue to harm the institution. His friends agreed. In December he resigned, effective with the installation of a new president after July 1899.

Chapman brought a number of things to the University: an expanded curriculum, larger student body in the collegiate ranks, more high-caliber in-state students, a faculty well qualified for their positions, an expanded library and librarian and the organization of such student activities as intercollegiate athletics and compulsory physical training.

—*Keith Richard*

The School on the Hill

THE UNIVERSITY OF OREGON MEDICAL SCHOOL

Organized in the autumn of 1887, the UO Medical School opened with Dr. Simeon E. Joseph as dean and C. C. Strong as secretary of the faculty. They began operations in a two-room wooden building on the grounds of Portland's Good Samaritan Hospital. The attendance was light, in the neighborhood of eighteen students, but the institution gained momentum in 1893 when a new two-story building (above) was erected on the corner of 23rd and Lovejoy Streets. In 1898 the school became a member of the American Medical Association and by 1902 enrollment had grown to eighty-nine students.
—Henry D. Sheldon

Shinn's freshman year, some students boarding with Grandma Fitch organized an athletic club, and the faculty gave them permission to use the assembly room of Deady Hall for a gymnasium. But when heavyweight boxing began to fill the front pages of the nation's newspapers, the faculty became alarmed about the possible pollution of academia by the vulgar fad; boxing gloves were removed from the gym.

Student bands were formed in some years, and presented programs in nearby towns. But these, and some innocuous private amusements, such as croquet, singing and church, were about the limits of the students' outside interests in George Shinn's day.

Students may not have had time for anything else. The University offered only two courses toward a degree, the "Classical" or the "Scientific." Both were grueling six-year programs. The first two years were devoted strictly to preparation, the last four to Latin, Greek or a modern foreign language, and the "exact sciences." Electives were unknown, though a bright student might be permitted to carry a heavier load of some favorite subject.

And the loads were already heavy. Each student could take no more than three or four subjects at a time, as each class met five times a week. Class periods were devoted to recitation and the assignment of the next day's work. All studying had to be done at home—no loitering was allowed around the University building, where the wood stoves in the classrooms at least took the chill out of the air.

Exactly how a future lawyer was expected to use the knowledge of Astronomy or Greek painfully gained by this old-school system was not considered important. The purpose of these heterogeneous classes was to "cultivate the mind in a general way by disciplining all the faculties…the mind may afterwards be applied to…any profession, art or business, and it will be able to work with precision, ease and power." This optimistic statement is from the University catalog of 1885.

This practice of "disciplining the faculties" was doomed by public response. It might have done well enough in the East, in the old days, but the growing Northwest needed a University that taught impoverished students what they needed to know, and did so in a hurry.

Villard Hall was opened in 1886, doubling the classroom space of the University, but public dislike of the old-school program was obvious. From an all-time high of sixteen graduates in 1883, the University produced only four graduates in 1885. A characteristic letter to a local newspaper complained that "the students…must plod on for four, five or six years…through the musty vaults of Greek and Roman mythology, to the utter disregard of what is going on about them."

A two-year course for elementary teachers called the "Normal" course was dropped in 1884. But now the reformers demanded a similar four-year, full credit course. Called the "English," because of the relaxed language requirements, this new course was adopted in 1886 over the bitter protests of faculty. Change was finally in the air; the jovial but conservative John Wesley Johnson resigned as president in 1893.

The new president, Charles Hiram Chapman, after his first look around, wrote sourly that the University had the "atmosphere of a petty theological seminary manned by superannuated ministers."

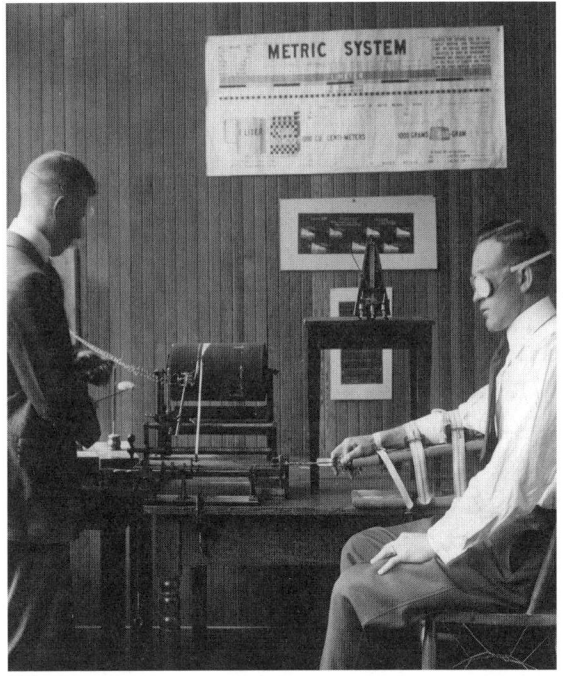

Studying the effect of mental fatigue at the turn of the century with the Mosso Ergograph.

As the Victorian era dragged stuffily onward, the already stilted relationship between male and female students became almost nonexistent. However impious his opinions of his senior faculty, Chapman had no intention of letting sex rear its unkempt head among the tidy flower-beds of academic endeavor. A new rule decreed that males and females should use different stairwells and classrooms. Young George Shinn, who had mused sentimentally ten years before over the pretty female student who wept as Prof. Johnson encouraged his flustered pupils, would have been hard put to find an outlet for romantic imaginings now.

A gymnasium had finally been built in 1890, and Chapman strongly approved of physical education; but the young ladies were reminded that their voluminous gymnasium suits were never to be worn outside that building. Football, eagerly anticipated, finally came to the campus in 1894, but Chapman decreed that no student who was merely mediocre in classes would be allowed on the team.

MILESTONES 1876–1900

1872
Legislature passes bill giving University to Eugene.

1873
J.H.D. Henderson donates land for campus.

1876
Regents elect first faculty. John Wesley Johnson named president. First students register October 16.

1876
First building completed.

1878
First graduation, five members in class.

1881
Henry Villard gives financial aid to University.

1884
LAW: Law school opens.

1886
Villard Hall completed.

MUS: The University of Oregon School of Music begins simply as the Department of Music in 1886. D.W. Coolidge serves as Chair.

Early woodcuts of the University campus show Deady Hall standing stark and alone on its slight elevation.... The problem of beautification was first raised by the students when the seniors of 1883 planted trees on the northwestern portion of campus. Many of these, mostly cedars, did not survive the dry season. Most of the present trees, firs, cedars, maples and palms, date from the next year and were put in by the University janitor under contract from the Regents.
—Henry D. Sheldon

1888
MUS: Mary E. McCornack begins tenure as Director of Conservatory of Music.

1891
Reflector, the first student newspaper, started.

1893
Charles Hiram Chapman succeeds Johnson as president. Judge Matthew Deady, first president of the Board of Regents, dies and Deady Hall named.

1894
First football game.

1895
First track team organized. First summer session held, near Seaside.

1896
LAW: First female graduate, Anna E. Wood, completes her studies.

1897
Oregon Monthly succeeds *Reflector* as newspaper.

1899
Frank Strong named third president.

AAA: School of Architecture & Allied Arts
BUS: College of Business
CAS: College of Arts & Sciences
ED: College of Education
J: School of Journalism & Communication
LAW: School of Law
MUS: School of Music

1876 – 1900

The first dormitory, Friendly Hall, was built in 1893, and gave both men and women an option to the sometimes dreary boarding houses a mile or more away from campus. The building was divided in half. The North entrance was for women, the South for men. The living quarters upstairs were separated by a wall—presumably a thick wall—and the downstairs sitting rooms were forbidden to members of the opposite sex except on Friday, Saturday and Sunday evenings.

Even so, the limited coed living experiment lasted only a year, and Friendly Hall became all male.

But the students themselves had begun to change, and the change was irreversible. The YMCA and YWCA appeared on campus in the 1890s, and about one-third of all students belonged to them, many for social reasons; and there were student societies for biology, the classics, music and chemistry. Strenuous students might join cheerful mixed parties in climbs up Spencer Butte or the Coburg Hills, or class picnics along the wild McKenzie. Then too, the Millrace had finally come into its own, and the unabashed romantics might opt for boat rides up the

S.H. FRIENDLY: REMEMBERING A UO FRIEND

When students petitioned the University to name their dormitory after Sampson H. Friendly, they were honoring a man who made his presence known on campus far beyond the board room. A self-made merchant, city councilman and mayor of Eugene, and twenty-year Regent of the University, Friendly never missed a football game nor an opportunity to quietly assist a student who was having trouble making ends meet.

Samson Friendly was born in New York in 1849 and traveled to the West Coast in his early twenties, arriving in Eugene virtually penniless. He got a job working in Goldsmith and Blanding, a general store, and within four years he had opened his own dry goods store in partnership with his brother-in-law. There two generations of students shopped for the "latest novelties in imported dress patterns" as well as "trimmings, silks, neckwear and clothing."

After the state legislature decreed that the city of Eugene would have to furnish land and a building if it were to become the site of the new state university, Friendly became a pivotal figure in that effort, raising funds during the week in order to pay the workers constructing Deady Hall on Saturday. He became a Regent in 1895 and continued to serve in that capacity until his death in 1915.

Accounts of his generosity, to individuals as well as the community at large, are numerous. A good play or concert would come to town, and Friendly would see to it that deserving students got tickets.

In a nearly full-page obituary, business associates and former employees all spoke of Friendly's personal kindness and dedication to the community.

"I think that Eugene owes it to the memory of Mr. Friendly to erect a suitable monument or do something of the kind," one said, "to let future generations know that we had such a citizen as he."

—*Bonnie Henderson*

wooded stream with a favorite member of the opposite sex and, amazingly, no chaperone at all.

Faculty rules multiplied in their attempts to enforce "morality." Students must not attend skating rinks, dancing clubs or public dances. Students must not attend *any* place of amusement from Monday morning until Friday night. Students must not leave town without faculty permission. Young ladies are forbidden to be at the station to meet the night train, unless they have the president's permission, etc.

One young man, apparently incorrigible, was solemnly "admonished that he may not return to the University until he has radically changed his relation to the tempting influences of Eugene."

In 1897 President Chapman, a fine schoolman but pompous and unable to understand local attitudes, was assailed by petitions, signed by many students and townspeople, asking for his removal and that of some other faculty members. Eventually

LUELLA CLAY CARSON: OF MORALS AND MANNERS

When James Greenfield, a student at the University of Oregon in 1890, walked Sue Dorris home from the ice cream social, he was ruefully conscious of a third presence. As he wrote in his diary, "We obeyed the instructions of Prof. Carson by not lingering at the gate over the pleasant time of the evening."

Luella Clay Carson, who had come to Oregon as professor of rhetoric and elocution, was also the social arbiter, preceptress of good breeding and the guardian of morals and manners of the University. Carson's specialties were written and oral composition. Her mission, as stated in a report to President Chapman, was to "impart the knowledge of the mother tongue, keep it unsullied and to see to it that it was used for good results." The degree to which she realized this impossible dream was surprising.

In her elocution classes, Carson was an effective drillmistress. She went far beyond "declamations" and taught her students to prepare and deliver original orations with appropriate style. Her "children," as she referred to her students, were led each year through a series of "Public Oratorials," culminating in intercollegiate contests.

As a natural adjunct of the principles of rhetoric and the fundamentals of public speaking, Carson taught the verities—truth, beauty, nobility. She was a committee of one that censored student publications and advised literary societies on social matters.

When control of the Department of English passed reluctantly from Carson's hands, she still reigned supreme as a teacher of composition and the preceptress of conduct and taste. The University recognized her defacto position and appointed her dean of women. She solicited information on codes of conduct from women's colleges in the East, hoping to learn the appropriate rules for cheering at football games, holding hands on campus and curfews.

When guides were not available, she set her own principles. For example, no girl on the campus was to play basketball—a sport Carson found "rough and unladylike."

After twenty-one years at Oregon, Carson was an institution, commanding respect and affection particularly among the alumni. She left the University in 1909 for the presidency of Mills College.

When Carson died in 1938 the recollection of her work was still strong in the minds of many of her old students. One of them, Edith Kerns Chambers, commented on "the loyalty to both truth and beauty which marked her service. A generation of her young people can testify to her careful training in orderly thinking which has been to many of them a deterrent to snap judgements and rampant prejudice."

—*Martin Schmitt and Keith Richard*

the petitions were rejected by the state as "frivolous," but this "era of bad feeling" left scars, and Chapman resigned in 1898. He was replaced by a Yale graduate, Frank Strong.

President Strong restructured the University into schools, and also became an innocent spectator to one of the more interesting results of the long bottling-up of youthful exuberance.

Back in the late '80s, male students, tired of grinding away the warm May weather in the classrooms, suddenly proclaimed one balmy spring morning "Skip Day" and set out to enjoy themselves. The idea caught on. The Junior Class, particularly, would unexpectedly pick a day in which they would refuse to go to classes and would do their best to make sure that nobody else did either. Noise, struggles between men of different classes, irreverent hilarity and minor property damage enlivened the staid campus scene.

In 1890 the faculty tried to forestall this vigorous young tradition by fixing one May Friday as the "Junior Exhibit," featuring student orations and other such bland stuff for the edification of students and the entertainment of townspeople.

Luella Clay Carson, professor of rhetoric and English, suggested that the Juniors confine their disruptive activities to an attempt to raise their class flag on a tower of Villard Hall and to defend that flag against their traditional rivals, the Sophomores.

As it turned out, Carson might best have kept quiet.

The annual "Junior Flag Rush" precipitated epic battles in which classes were disrupted, professors' nerves shattered, and academic serenity murdered as the Juniors took on all comers in ritualized and noisy battle. Black eyes, bruises and contusions, occasional broken bones and fractured friendships marked the course of battle for the Junior flag.

Junior women, working for weeks in secret locations, would lovingly stitch a huge silken banner in their class colors, emblazoned with the class year. Persistent Sophomores would dog the Juniors' heels, trying to discover their flag's location so as to steal it before the big day. Hiding places were changed and all sorts of elaborate ruses were employed to get the flag up. The Sophomores and Seniors tried to circumvent such strategy by waylaying stray Juniors and tying them up to keep them out of the battle.

For once a flag was up, a battle royal ensued as men of other classes attempted to pull it down. If the flag were lost, a shameful substitute had to be quickly made, for the flag customarily formed a backdrop for the Junior orators at the exhibit that evening.

> *The University provided a few set occasions for acquaintanceship. New students each year were welcomed at an informal occasion known as the walk-around. Later in the year, there were joint open meetings of the literary societies. The faculty frowned on theatricals, and dancing was tabooed.*
> —Henry D. Sheldon

Early Sports

The first football game.

The first football team, on their way to an undefeated season.

Athletic policy was established initially with a men's baseball team organized in 1877. Their first intercurricular game was played in Eugene against Monmouth College. The visitors promptly destroyed any visions of an Oregon baseball dynasty— Monmouth led 17-0 after one inning.

Early track and field had a much more encouraging start. In 1895, a team was hastily formed to compete in a state-wide collegiate meet at Salem's Willamette University. With virtually no training, the trackmen handily defeated their rivals. They also won meets in 1896, 1898, 1899 and 1900. With the help of UO's first track coach, W. O. "Dad" Trine, the Oregon track and field dynasty had begun.

While the track program won its place in the athletic scene through its phenomenal success, football was the most popular sport of the time. In the beginning, football was coached by enthusiastic local volunteers, starting with businessman Cal Young. It is unclear when the University's first intercollegiate football game was played. The 1902 yearbook placed the game in 1893, while other accounts place the game in March of 1894. The score was also disputed, although all records indicate that the Eugene team won by a landslide.

The rest of the 1893 (or 1894) season was less than successful, but the gridders were not discouraged. The team came back in 1895 to record the school's only undefeated and untied season.

> *Football rules and procedures were not standardized in the Pacific Northwest and things often got rowdy. Two different games between the University of Oregon and Oregon Agricultural College ended in riots, yells of derision, hoots and cat calls. Charges of trickery and the drafting of nonstudents were frequently made.*
> —Henry D. Sheldon

By this time, the Oregon–Oregon State rivalry was well on its way to current levels of intensity. A 44-0 rout of Oregon Agricultural College (OSU's original name) avenged the previous year's loss to the UO's ultimate intrastate rival, and the Oregon men continued their dominance over their Corvallis opponents well into the 1900s.

—*Bruce Dworshak*

The brawl might take place around the tall flagpole just west of Villard Hall, or the Juniors might barricade themselves on top of Deady or Villard Halls, playing a dangerous game of king of the mountain to defend their flag as it floated from one of the towers. Incredibly, there is no record of anyone getting killed in those sieges.

The day before Flag Rush in 1899, the class of 1900 took possession of the flagpole, ran their flag up, and then fastened a large dry-goods box halfway up. Junior Walter B. Dillard took up residence in this elevated perch, and legend has it that he was provisioned through the long night by classmate Mamie McAlister, who stood below and tossed doughnuts up to him.

Daylight revealed him perched aloft like a dyspeptic crow in its nest, peering suspiciously down at passersby and prepared to repel boarders with a water hose. He saved his class flag, but three years later the same strategem was to backfire; the Sophomores overwhelmed and tied up every Junior except the two in the elevated box, then stuck a fire hose out of an upper window of Villard and soaked the besieged guards into surrender.

President Strong's introduction to this cheerful little event, the Flag Rush, apparently came with the notable battle of Deady Hall, May 3, 1900.

The Juniors discovered that some "wretch of the lower orders" had removed the halyards from the flagpole. Undaunted, they set their purple and gold banner flying from a tower atop Deady Hall and barricaded the stairwells. Although all the other classes ganged up on them, they eventually triumphed.

Skirmishes rolled up and down the hallways of Deady and spilled over into the space between Deady and Villard. Friend and foe alike were trampled underfoot in the enthusiasm of the occasion, the noise was terrific and classes were pretty well shot for the day.

Frederick S. Dunn, professor of Latin, was to recall in later years the plight of several professors, himself among them, who were trying to reach Deady at the time.

"Never shall I forget," he wrote, "the rout and the sweat of the battle that raged in the open between Deady and Villard and through the hallways of Deady…."

Looking out over the hurly-burly, Dunn saw President Strong staring back at him from his own classroom in Villard, and the expression on the president's face was hardly amused.

While UO men enjoyed success on the gridiron and the track field, women had a harder time finding athletic competition. There is a photo of the women's basketball team of 1900, but no record of their play—or of any other organized women's sports during the early years of UO.

Just after 1900, the disruptive Junior Flag Rush, top, gave way to the campus improvements of University Day.

At the Exhibition that evening, Strong opened the exercises by remarking, "So this is Junior Day…at least I have been told that it is. The smoke of battle having cleared away, I take the occasion to congratulate the Regents that the buildings are still standing."

An official attempt to defuse the Flag Rush followed, but was not particularly successful.

The final straw came in 1904, when the Juniors took the roof of Villard Hall the evening before the Flag Rush, stocked it with provisions and camping gear, set their flag flying, then chained down and padlocked the trap door leading to the roof. They settled down to wait out the next day in triumph, but the Sophomores cut down a telephone pole to use as a ram on the trap door, filched some ladders from the fire department to scale the roof—six stories up—and the battle was joined. Eventually, the flag was torn up for souvenirs by the victors—and the captured defenders "taken for a ride"—via wagon—and turned loose in the country for a long walk back.

No casualties—except the smashed trap door—were reported, but the "fun" associated with Junior Day had progressed to the point that even the participants began to look forward to the event with apprehension.

The next year, 1905, with the prompting of President Prince Lucien Campbell (nicknamed "Good Prince Campbell" by students), a truce was called. The old Junior Day became University Day, in which students of all classes banded together to clean up and improve the campus. As events were added year by year, this eventually became the Junior Weekend, replete with dances, picnics, sports events and capped by the glorious Canoe Fete.

But the demise of the Junior Flag Rush was more than just the end of a barbaric tradition; student attitudes and student lifestyles were changing with the easing of old restrictions.

The old debating and literary societies, once the center of student social life, had quietly faded away around the turn of the century, along with the orations which had satisfied the local yeomanry's idea of a proper university.

It was the beginning of a new era in student life, with new customs, new problems, a new spirit. George Shinn, the green young frontiersman from the wilds of the Grande Ronde, would have been lost on the lively, sophisticated campus of 1905.

The rough childhood of the University of Oregon had ended.

THOMAS CONDON: MISSIONARY TURNED SCIENTIST

Thomas Condon was one of the three members of the collegiate faculty of the University when it opened in 1876. Professor of geology and natural history, he was the favorite among students and the public alike, the best known of the three and the only one to achieve something of a national reputation.

He had come to his field of geology and the professorship by an unlikely and circuitous route. As a preacher, he was sent to Oregon in 1853 by the Home Missionary Society of the Congregational Church. His long-time interest in science had largely given way to his duties as a minister. But out on a bluff above the river where he sought privacy and solitude while preparing his sermons, he kicked over a rock and discovered a fossil leaf of extraordinary beauty and detail. He soon had the town in a fever of activity, collecting specimens for him or for themselves—boys, citizens, miners and army troops on assignment in the field.

Condon knew the vocabulary of geology and understood the processes of geological change. Rejecting the commonly accepted biblical literalism of his day, he pushed back the geological history of Oregon some millions of years.

At the UO, Condon taught a wide variety of courses, a total of fourteen in 1878–79 alone, including Physical Features of the Earth, Mineralogy, Physiology, History of the United States, Geology, Botany, International Law and Rhetoric. He drilled his students on geography, names of rocks, classification of plants and flowers and events in history. His advanced class in geography culminated in an exam where students picked an assignment from a hat and proceeded to draw the named continent, state or sea on the blackboard and identify rivers, lakes, mountains and bordering territories.

His classroom was crowded with cabinets and tables containing rocks, minerals, fossils, bones, insects and flowers. Professor Condon also enjoyed field trips. In the first year he took his class, accompanied by a number of citizens, on foot and on horseback, in buggies and lumber wagons, along the rough road to Spencer Butte for a lecture and picnic. Standing atop the butte, he pointed out features of the landscape, advancing his theory that the valley had once been covered by the sea.

Condon's quick intelligence and marvelous imagination were curbed by his meager background, isolation from other scientists and heavy teaching course load. Still, he was respected and honored by several scientists and was without peer in the Pacific Northwest. Retired from teaching well past his seventieth year, Condon sat down to write a geological history of Oregon. When he died in 1906, former University President Chapman wrote, "Oregon loses the most interesting character who has thus far appeared among her teachers."

—*Robert D. Clark*

Women's basketball, 1917.

Class of '26 Painting the "O" as Frosh

Collecting materials for the Freshman Bonfire.

1900-1929

The Rowdy Ragtime Years

omebody was going to pull the old cannonball stunt again.

Since the dormitory (later Friendly Hall) was separated into north and south wings, and one wing's denizens were more studious than the other, it was natural that a cheerful feud should develop; equally natural that the faculty should assign a young instructor to live in the dorm and try to hold down the carnage; and inevitable, of course, that the instructor should become the victim of the old cannonball stunt.

The cannonball had been kicking around the dorm as long as anyone could remember. On this particular night, someone sneaked it down to the basement, heated it up in the furnace, then smuggled it up to the top floor. Everyone was safely abed when the hot iron ball was started rolling down the steep stairwells—Ba-LUMP! Rumble-rumble...Ba-LUMP! Rumble-rumble... Ba-LUMP!

By the time the ball had completed its stately, thunderous descent, everyone was awake; and at the bottom of the stairs, an indignant, nightshirted instructor ran out and thoughtlessly grabbed up the hot cannonball...then a sharp yell and a final thud put a period to the night's symphony and filled some miscreant with silent glee.

This was the University of Oregon campus at the turn of the century—456 students, half a dozen buildings, a nervous faculty who saw the ironbound discipline of Victorian days slipping irretrievably away and a dormitory full of young roughnecks who dearly loved a bit of fun.

Not that students were actually wild, of course; the tradition of the staid '90s was still too close and they were unused to the

by Walter Wentz

New freedoms, pranks and a budding social life marked the transition between the Victorian Era and the Great Depression.

The Rowdy Ragtime Years

Maypole Dance, 1917.

taste of freedom. It would take a couple of decades for them to warm up for the Jazz Age. But this Ragtime Era of the campus soon developed its own character.

The Commandment against fraternizing with the other gender had become a dead letter. Most of the men and all the women were still living off campus; but at least they could now study in the same room and there were even public dances to which students went openly. Not having much experience at dancing, they had to sneak lessons in private.

The year 1900 marked the beginning of student independence. The Associated Students were organized that year, mainly to finance social events with the first incidental fees. The *Oregon Weekly*, under its first editor, Clifton (Pat) McArthur '01, began publication. By 1920 it would become the *Daily Emerald*. The first University fraternity chapter, Sigma Nu, was founded but the first sorority was still four years away.

Recreation for proper young students included hikes up the local hills, junkets to the McKenzie River and picnics at the maple grove near Hayden Bridge or Abraham's Mill, a scenic water wheel. Farther upstream was O'Brien's, offering weekend fishing, home cooking and fresh air.

Tennis had been played in a local barnyard in the '90s, but now students graded proper courts on campus, and two clubs, the Muckers and Nonpareils, played mixed matches.

Recreation for proper young students included hikes up the local hills, junkets to the McKenzie River and picnics at the maple grove near Hayden Bridge or Abraham's Mill, a scenic water wheel.

With dancing and parties came music—including barbershop quartets.

1900–1929

Football was becoming almost a religion on the nation's campuses, and the new Kincaid Field (located where Chapman and Condon Halls now stand) replaced the pioneer gridiron across 13th. The new field sloped down to the street, and a foot of water and mud made play a bit awkward on that side.

Hosts of University traditions were springing up; most were rites of passage designed to introduce the raw young freshmen to the campus. Hazing was rough, despite repeated faculty warnings, and, among male students at least, involved "bathtubbing," paddling and various other demeaning or even painful ordeals.

The freshmen of the year 1902 were the first to wear the "green lid," or frosh cap, as a badge of servitude. Forbidden them by tradition were corduroys (reserved for sophomores), pipes (for juniors only) or sombreros (for seniors).

Not only were they expected to conform to established student customs, such as extinguishing all tobacco before crossing the board fence around the campus, but rigid restrictions were placed on dating, drinking, speaking and attitude. These restrictions were posted everywhere on hair-raising placards, listing the grisly punishments to be inflicted upon the miserable carcasses of frosh transgressors. And it was taken for granted that they had transgressed, were transgressing, or would transgress and therefore might as well be annihilated anyway.

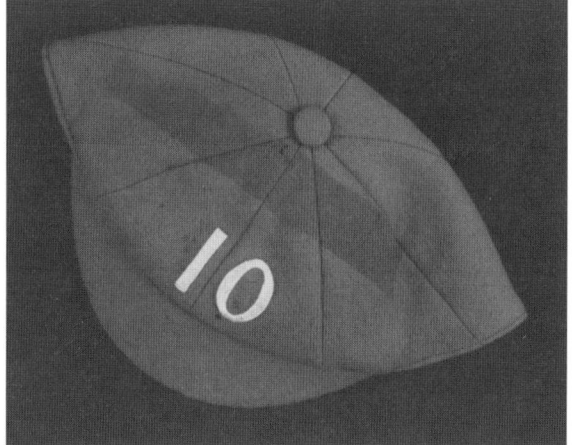

Frosh cap, 1910.

The freshmen of the year 1902 were the first to wear the "green lid," or frosh cap, as a badge of servitude.

President Prince Lucien Campbell arrived in 1902 and soon became "Good Prince Lucien" to the students. Learned, diplomatic, diffident almost to the point of awkwardness, Campbell had a knack for making himself liked by everyone.

It was at his urging that the oldest and most violent tradition, the Junior Flag Rush, was transformed into University Day in May 1905, when all students worked on campus improvements.

The Millrace had been the recreational center for the campus since the '90s, when young couples or groups, dispensing with the chaperone, rowed sedately along the wood stream in the awkward, flat-bottomed skiffs of the day. There was a good deal of drifting about under the stars, great effusions of sentimental poetry and gruff announcements of curfews by the faculty. Student verse, prose, photography and artwork, even a play, all

Treble Cleft (sic) Club, 1901.

Kappa Sigma Seniors.

The first sorority, Beta Epsilon, appeared in 1904. In six years there would be a total of fifteen frats and house clubs, eight sororities, and women's dorms would finally appear on the campus.

revealed the fascination of the lovely little stream flowing by the campus. Not until the advent of the light, maneuverable canoe, however, would the Millrace enter into its full glory.

It is written that Ralph Bacon '06 and Edward Lister '07 were the first to launch canoes on the Race, in 1903; it is also written that they were the first to attempt midwinter canoeing and to sneak home by the back streets, shivering, sneezing and dripping wet.

The new craft gave a great impetus to romance and soon every barn on the Race housed canoes. In a few years there were nearly 100 on the stream—private, student-owned, or belonging to boat liveries.

So important, in fact, was the Millrace that when the University reversed an old policy and began encouraging fraternal organizations (because of the housing shortage in a growing Eugene), most fraternities and sororities chose to settle along the stream.

Local landlords were reluctant to rent houses to student groups, and they had to find lodging where they could. Sigma Nu had to live in a hotel for a time. The first sorority, Beta Epsilon, appeared in 1904. In six years there would be a total of fifteen frats and house clubs, eight sororities, and women's dorms would finally appear on the campus.

Football and track kept booming in a big way, as Trainer Bill Hayward turned out a succession of fine teams. Kincaid Field

Frank Strong
President 1899-1902

"The state university, if it fulfills its function, must become the center of the intellectual life of the state. It has no right to exist unless it becomes the center of power from which radiates streams of influence touching every part of the commonwealth."

Frank Strong wrote that in December 1899, shortly after he became the third president of the University of Oregon. He was a New Yorker with a doctorate in history from Yale. He had never been west before, and he was a little appalled at the primitive conditions he found. He complained particularly of the flea-infested hotels and train coaches. But he was also amazed at the young state's beauty. And he had the strongest opinions that a university should be a citizen of the state.

Strong reported to the Regents that a bachelor's degree granted at Oregon was not equal to that of Harvard or Yale, and that several factors caused this: the low number of high schools in Oregon, the lack of an adequate library, up-to-date laboratories, museums, art collections or a graduate school.

Strong was bothered by the fact that so many male graduates of the University entered the ministry. He saw it as a weakness that the liberal education of the University was dominated by the classics. He proposed changes that would produce men and women for a variety of tasks in society.

The new president tackled the responsibilities of his office with all the energy his 6'5" frame could muster. Strong asked the Regents

Strong's administration was open to students and his residence was a place for student parties. His bass voice and piano playing were added to the local glee club. He pushed for the football team's first out-of-state game and for the debate team and glee club to travel to Washington State.

to allow him to establish departments with deans—something Johnson and Chapman had repeatedly and unsuccessfully proposed. The Regents endorsed Strong's policy. With more freedom to hire faculty, Strong brought some outstanding individuals to the campus. He was allowed to hire a registrar, a steward and a secretary; these moves freed him from some of the administrative tasks of his predecessors.

Strong was given permission to inspect Oregon high schools and make sure their curricula met University standards. With the help of Henry Sheldon, professor of philosophy and education, he devised a plan for accrediting high schools and admitting their graduates to the University.

The library grew in size through Strong's efforts. He had it moved into a wing of the men's dormitory (now Friendly Hall) and increased book purchases. Definite hours were established for the library, and the faculty was expected to make assignments that required its use.

In 1901, the first summer session for public school teachers was held. In 1902 the Regents voted to discontinue it. Strong protested vigorously, and this became a factor in his decision to resign that same year. In his last report to the Regents, Strong emphasized the need for greater expansion of the curriculum, faculty and funding. The Board voted to have his written report stricken from the record.

During the Strong administration, a faculty of considerable intellectual strength was built, and the student body grew as did the curriculum. More of the students who in the past left the state now came to Eugene for university training. Despite his disagreements with the Regents, Strong contributed to their education on the subject of a university. It is partially because of this that the fourth president, Prince Lucien Campbell, was to have the success he had in administering the University.

—*Keith Richard*

The Rowdy Ragtime Years

had a new grandstand, erected by volunteer student labor, but the school had no characteristic mascot as yet. In 1907, Cary Loosely '09 and Bug Merryman '09 provided one: a goat.

Billy was a real, live, brassbound goat, with a head like iron and an ingrown disposition. Decked out in his own "O" sweater for games, he looked mean enough to clear the gridiron by himself, but he preferred to terrorize students instead.

He was stabled on the third floor, south end of the dorm, and invested the building with his own wild, peculiar fragrance. The campus lawns were his pasture, and his favorite roosting place was the front steps of the brand-new library, Fenton Hall. After several disastrous collisions, students bent on study learned to sneak in the side entrance, avoiding the lordly goat's private stair.

"COLONEL" BILL HAYWARD: DEAN OF AMERICAN TRACK

In a 1903 letter to President Campbell, a colleague of Bill Hayward's wrote: "Hayward is now looked upon as one of the best trainers in the Northwest and I think he can develop a winning team for the University of Oregon." His recommendation couldn't have been more correct—or more of an understatement.

William Louis Hayward—known to most as "Colonel Bill"—became the undisputed dean of American track coaches, a mentor to dozens of Olympians and, above all, the father of track and field at the University of Oregon. Hayward coached at Oregon for almost forty-five years, but his status as a beloved campus legend, an international sports figure and the epitome of sportsmanship and clean competition was established well before his retirement in 1947.

Hayward, originally from Detroit, came to Oregon to coach after an extraordinary athletic career of his own. Internationally known as a runner, Hayward also excelled professionally at boxing, lacrosse, rowing and wrestling. In all of these, Hayward held "twins of victory" above all else: the will to win and the spirit of competition.

Under his tutelage, Oregon athletes found a new level of success. Dan Kelly, a world-record-holding miler, traveled to the 1906 Olympics, and Hayward came along at his own expense, only to be recruited to be an assistant coach for the U.S. team once he'd arrived in London. During the 1912 Games in Stockholm, the German team was so impressed with him that they asked him to coach their team in 1916—an assignment that was cancelled after the beginning of World War II. In all, Hayward coached at six Olympiads, often with Oregon athletes on his team.

His impact on the Oregon campus was felt just as deeply as his influence on the world athletic stage. A consummate sportsman and coach, Hayward, the "Grand old man of Oregon Athletics," was involved at every level, from training Olympic athletes to bringing water in buckets out to thirsty football players at the quarter. Hayward was such a common sight on the gridiron, in fact, that when the University purchased a steam-powered water cart, it was instantly dubbed "Hayward Junior." He was also forever inventing braces and pads to help injured athletes, cobbling devices out of foam rubber and rivets to take the pressure off a cracked collarbone or a twisted knee.

Hayward's most permanent legacy is twofold: the tradition of excellence in track and field that he started almost a century ago, and the field that bears his name. Maintaining its aura as the Carnegie Hall of track and field, Hayward Field has been the site of countless world and national records over the years. As one of the most famous track and field facilities in the nation, it is a fitting tribute to a man who devoted his career to Oregon athletics.

"He loved Oregon," a colleague of Hayward's said upon his death, "and Oregon loved him."

—*Jessica MacMurray*

1900–1929

Cap Briggs, the paunchy, walrus-whiskered groundskeeper, had a running feud with Billy—and Cap did most of the running. Finally he inquired if anyone would greatly miss the irascible beast if he should happen to accidentally leap into a passing farmer's wagon and get hauled away. Apparently nobody minded, and shortly the University was without a mascot; while the library's front steps were open to the public once more.

This prewar era from 1907 onwards was a period complete of itself—students were becoming cocky, flip and sophisticated. They spoke the slang immortalized in George Ade's *Fables in Slang*, using such catch phrases as "I gotcher, Steve," and "Yea Bo." Males began smoking pipes, though, as always, knocking them out as they crossed the stile onto the sacred turf of the Old 'Varsity.

In the old days, even to be seen going into a saloon was to be expelled; by 1909 a group of students drinking in the old dorm was merely "excluded from the privileges of the Dormitory." This feeble gesture was apparently all that the faculty could make stick.

This was the hearty era of good local brewed beer at a nickel a schooner, in convivial sawdust-floored saloons where the patrons, in amateur harmony, provided their own music. Eugene, troubled by religious qualms despite the fact that it had more saloons than churches, became involved in the local option nonsense, and voted itself dry, then wet, then dry again. With the drying up of Eugene, those on pleasure bent had only to catch

> *Hayward Field is one of the most famous track and field facilities in the nation. It has been the site for three Olympic Trials and eight NCAA Championships, the last of which occurred in 1996. A 14,200-seat facility, it has served as the UO Track and Field home since 1921. Hayward also doubled as the home of the football team until Autzen Stadium opened in 1967.*

A "Slow Race" on Hayward Field, 1914.

> *From 1920 on, there was notable growth of the graduate school. In 1902, there were five master's degrees granted; in 1926 there were thirty-five. Their distribution included: English, eight; Education, six; Mathematics, four; Psychology, three; Romance Languages, Geology, Chemistry and Physics, two each. Geology led the way with the first Ph.D. in 1926 followed by Education and Biology.*
>
> —Henry D. Sheldon

the trolley to Springfield where there was a saloon on every corner; then ho for the midnight trolley and the clattering ride home, and the headache next morning.

In justice, it must be pointed out that the great majority of students frequented such places as the College Side Inn, that high-ceilinged, cozy cavern just across the street from campus which sold nothing stronger than Coca-Cola.

In November of 1910, with 634 students, both the campus and Eugene were straining at the seams. Horseless carriages were increasing the glut of traffic on the roads, and the faculty "respectfully requested the Regents to take steps to prevent excessive traffic of wagons, motorcycles… and especially automobiles, that endanger the lives of students and constantly disturb with indescribable noise all recitations in buildings adjacent to the road." Despite the respectful requests of the faculty, the problem of traffic on 13th lived on to the venerable age of sixty years, and it was finally eliminated in 1970 by action of the students themselves.

In 1914, the Great War which was to devastate Europe was still remote. Students complained that an arc lamp installed over the new Senior Bench inhibited romance and despite official disapproval of "Millracing," ducking stools (chairs to which the

IRENE HAZARD GERLINGER: FIRST LADY OF FUNDRAISING

Originally from Portland, Irene Hazard Gerlinger served from 1915 to 1929 as the only woman on the University Board of Regents. Nothing was too small to engage her attention—she pursued the collection of Indian arrowheads with the same vigor that she lobbied at the State Legislature. But her most spectacular undertaking was the coordination of a campaign to raise $100,000 for the construction of a women's building on campus.

The movement had begun in 1913 under the aegis of M. Ruth Guppy, dean of women, and the Women's League of the University. Gerlinger took it up in 1915 with the vow that the results would be "the finest possible building" for female physical education activities and for University and community social activities.

Individual donations ranged from $1 to $1,000 and more. Some were the result of a series of lectures by campus notables, others were pledged as "bricks" for the Women's Memorial Gymnasium at 25¢ each. Gerlinger traveled extensively to visit colleges with similar buildings and to search out the most elegant possible furnishings for the Alumni Hall in the building. Ultimately, the building was named in her honor—Gerlinger Hall.

Gerlinger's energetic commitment to fundraising continued with her appointment as chair of the finance committee responsible for raising the more than $200,000 needed to house the Murray Warner Collection of Oriental Art. Begun in 1923, the drive was completed in 1930. $220,000 had been contributed by University friends, alumni and citizens of the state. With matching monies allocated from the state, construction could begin.

—Hope Hughes Pressman

Prince Lucien Campbell
President 1902–1925

Those who knew President Prince Lucien Campbell described him as a scholar, leader, founder—too modest over his own accomplishments, strong because of his faith in others.

Those who were personally acquainted with him said that his greatest contributions to Oregon were the constant expression of his supreme faith in democracy and his keen appreciation of pioneer ideals. In the most trying times of the University, when possibly the educational results seemed more important than the institutions of democracy, he replied, "The remedy for the evils of democracy lies in more democracy."

Such was the philosophy of the man who was to guide the University through its period of greatest expansion. Prince L. Campbell was born in 1861 in a small Missouri town, but his parents moved to Montana shortly after. He spent the next few years in a pioneer environment of a typical old-time western town. When he was eight years old the family came to Oregon where his father, Thomas Campbell, eventually assumed the position of president of the Christian College at Monmouth.

Young Campbell completed his studies there at the age of eighteen. For three years he assisted his father, teaching certain elementary courses, then in 1882 he left the west, entered Harvard as a sophomore and completed the requirements for a bachelor's degree.

Campbell returned to Monmouth to teach and soon became known in state education circles for his speaking ability and personal charm. In May 1902, he was elected to the University of Oregon as president. It was Campbell's intent from the beginning to build harmony, not only within the faculty but between students and faculty as well. He spent his time and energy dealing with personalities. His letters show interest in small personal problems—finding a job for a student without funds; whether fees should be returned to a thrifty mother whose son had withdrawn—the president dealt in person with these small details. At one time he taught a class in freshman ethics.

It is hard to realize how small the University was when President Campbell took over in 1902. At that time there were only about 250 students and the needs of the University were satisfied with an annual appropriation of $47,500. At the time of his death, enrollment was reaching 3,000 and annual appropriations amounted to $966,000. The campus increased from four buildings to thirty-eight.

During the twenty-three years that he was in office the University made steady gains, not only in enrollment and physical stature, but also in faculty. President Campbell made frequent trips to the East Coast to interview prospective teachers for appointment.

The continuous battle for funds made planning difficult. Moving to overcome this obstacle, President Campbell took the lead in appealing to citizens of the state and the legislature to provide for continuing taxes to meet annual financial needs beyond what was covered by appropriations.

Shortly after the campaign to raise funds had culminated in the attainment of his goal, Campbell became ill. For the last two years of his life the actual work was carried on by an executive board. It was said of him after his death that "His was the spirit of the artist applied to the affairs of life."
—*Bill Frye*

> *In 1902, the University consisted of schools of liberal arts and engineering in Eugene and law and medicine in Portland. Under Campbell, many schools and departments were added including music, education, journalism, both business and architecture, and sociology.*

unlucky were tied and dunked in the water) bloomed in the back yards of fraternity houses.

George W. Davis '18 has written of those last few years before the war. No student owned a car, though the big spender might hire a horse and buggy before an important dance. Dancing was big at Oregon, with special college steps and all:

Senior Class Kid Ball, 1926.

> *Oregon danced and put on great style…the roughneck of the evening was a one-stepper who wound himself up to the point of doing a spiral fantasy. Some of us are now wearing false teeth due to this type of pest. He would clutch his partner to him, rush forth at great speed, and at the most crowded spot on the floor, go round and round, left arm straight out, coat tails on the same plane. And when his partner's hair began to loosen, he'd rush on for the next spasm. They did the "grape-vine" too and used to be real rough by bending their partner way back….*

The unique spirit of the place was fostered by its traditions:

> *"Hello" was a great word when I trod the campus. We said it to everyone…. Knowing everyone on the campus, at least well enough to speak to, is the redeeming advantage of a small college. It insures good spirit…. And Oregon was strong for tradition. The spirit…was conveyed and re-conveyed from man to man. It was for the sake of the University that men adhered to rule or forced a classmate to get into step if he were out. Studying Oregon's past traditions, her ideals, her codes, can materially help the oncoming class.*

Handshaking was also part of the school traditions.

> *Everybody "shook" every place—going away, coming back, before breakfast, on the campus, down town. Even the girls gripped hands as aptly as the men….*

Due to the traditional training, both hellos and extra-firm handshakes were supposed to convey real cordiality, and, apparently, University grads years apart could recognize each other by this strong Oregon grip.

The major home football game of the season was an event requiring much ritual preparation and spiritual priming. Upon the freshmen fell the task of guarding the "O" on Skinner Butte to prevent its defilement with other school colors in the nights before the game, and the strenuous job of the Freshman Bonfire.

The building of the bonfire took weeks, in which the frosh scoured the country round for any scrap lumber that wasn't

The student newspaper, University of Oregon Weekly, *became more important as an organ of opinion as the student body increased in number. In 1909–1910, it was published twice a week and rechristened the* Oregon Emerald. *Soon afterward, in 1912, it was changed into a tri-weekly, and then into a daily in 1920.*

On and Around the Gridiron

The 1916 team practices beside Johnson Hall (top); on the field at the 1917 Rose Bowl.

Oregon's second quarter-century of sport rivaled any in the country. Despite its limited scale, the young University enjoyed some of the finest moments in sport thanks to two men in particular.

The first was Colonel Bill Hayward, trainer of all athletic teams for as long as anyone could remember. The second, Hugo Bezdek, was a young, native Austrian who learned the fundamentals of football at the University of Chicago. Bill and Bez, as the students addressed them, were two generations apart but equal to the task of getting the most from their athletes. Both coached the most dominant teams the West Coast had known up to that time.

Hayward's track men set the precedent of quality performance still expected today from the popular Eugene sport. Oregon's first track All-American, world record holder Dan Kelly, was coached by Hayward to record times in the sprints. Kelly won the silver medal in the 1908 London Olympics (broad jump) and still ranks high on the UO's all-time records list.

Hugo Bezdek came to Eugene to coach football full time in 1913 and turned the program around. His third season's (7-2) record was the winningest in the school's short football history.

Training was the secret to his team's success. With the help of Bill Hayward's conditioning programs, Oregon fielded the finest physically tuned team of the era. In 1917, the hard work paid off with a 14-0 victory over Pennsylvania in the Rose Bowl.

Experts claim that World War I was the only thing that kept Oregon from dominating West Coast football for four consecutive years. American involvement escalated just before the 1917 fall season, and the team's ranks were decimated.

With the end of the war, virtually the entire team returned, bringing winning football along with it. The 1919 team compiled a 5-1 record and became the first college team to play in back-to-back Rose Bowls.

—*Bruce Dworshak*

The Rowdy Ragtime Years

Freshman Bonfire, 1914.

nailed down. The night before the big game, when the huge pyre was lit—well, let the 1917 *Oregana* describe it:

> *Booming into full flame, the giant torch lit up the whole neighborhood and drove speakers and rooters further from the holocast. [sic] On the arms of a full wind the blaze swang far out over the gridiron, while myriads of sparks hissed and showered into the street.*

The flickering light lit and reddened the black field, the black stands and the black thousands who tramped and stamped there. Speakers rose, cheered and battled with their voices against the howling of the wind and the roar of flames behind them.

By 1915, the big game of the season had become Homecoming, for which old grads from years past returned to the alma mater.

In the same year, a proposal to establish military training on the campus aroused sharp public protests. But then came the sinking of the *Lusitania*, and public opinion abruptly reversed itself. As America slid into the war, a department of military science was founded at the UO, and military training was required of all males except Bible students.

Heading the Student Army Training Corps (SATC) was Colonel John Leader of the British army, one of the most flamboyant characters ever to hit the campus.

Practically a stereotype of the young British officer—trim, erect, with a flashing grin and a thin mustache—Colonel John was of Irish descent, had knocked about all over the world, and had been a translator of German, Chinese and Japanese before leading his Irish troops at Somme, and there receiving the wound that put him out of active service.

His service at the University was active enough; arriving to find students drilling with wooden guns in a hodgepodge of makeshift uniforms, he soon had SATC worked into a military concern.

Col. John Leader.

Democratic, understanding, humorous, but a disciplinarian, the "Jazzy General" as he was called became immensely popular with everyone, including his cadets. He set them to drilling, shooting, studying and digging up the empty field where McArthur Court stands today, making trenches, dugouts, first-aid and lookout stations and barbed-wire entanglements until that corner of campus resembled the Western Front.

University men enlisted in the regular services so rapidly that classes were cancelled, fraternity houses closed up and the administration granted credit for unfinished courses. More than 2,000 University students and alumni enlisted; a University ambulance corps was in France in the summer of 1918.

Of the forty-seven Oregon men who died during World War I, far more were victims of disease than of German fire. The terrible influenza epidemic of 1918, which killed uncounted thousands worldwide, struck the University with great force. Two empty fraternity houses became emergency infirmaries and dormitories also sheltered the stricken. Nonstudents attending summer military encampments on the campus were affected also.

Orange posters were everywhere, warning against spitting, coughing, to wash often, to use one's own toothbrush. In one week of October, ten servicemen died in Eugene.

SATC was disbanded with the end of the war, but ROTC was instated, and a permanent infirmary was the main benefit of the war for the University.

The University was growing madly. In 1919 there were 1,839 students, almost double the number in 1915. Many were soldiers and sailors back to finish interrupted studies.

Darle Seymour '22 was one of those returning, accepting the $60 bonus for ex-servicemen and spending it on clothes and gear to make a brave splash on campus.

"It was a lovely time to live, to be in college," Seymour recalled. The spirit of the times was buoyant; there would be no more wars, and the new technology would bring a good life to everyone. "We thought we had a free ride," Seymour said.

The Student Army Training Corps.

He set them to drilling, shooting, studying and digging up the empty field where McArthur Court stands today, making trenches, dugouts, first-aid and lookout stations… until that corner of campus resembled the Western Front.

The Rowdy Ragtime Years

There was an amazing flowering of the national culture and, at the same time, the college culture emerged full-blown, along with Prohibition and the Roaring Twenties.

This was a time of revamping and jazzing up of old customs, of silent movies, high teas, innumerable dances, canoes gliding again on the Millrace, the throaty rumble of the big yellow Stutz Bearcat down at the Phi Delta house.

Hayward Field, a magnificent new gridiron, was opened in 1919 in time for the annual battle with Oregon Agricultural College (later renamed Oregon State). For Homecoming games, the Frosh Bonfire was now preceded by a serpentine "Noise Parade" from downtown Willamette Street to the campus, involving scores of torches, flares, an ungodly amount of yelling and, as years went by, steamrollers, roaring saws and anything else that would make a racket. Older Eugenians succinctly describe this event as "hellish."

Junior Weekend, near the end of the school year, was now dominated by the glorious Canoe Fete, and increasingly huge

Major Facilities and Additions * 1900–1929	
Name	Year
Lawrence Hall	1901
Fenton Hall	1905
Johnson Hall	1915
Gilbert Hall	1916
Hendricks Hall	1917
Hayward W. Grandstand	1919
Music Building	1920
Education Building	1921
Gerlinger Hall	1921
Susan Campbell Hall	1921
Allen Hall	1922
Condon Hall	1925
Hayward E. Grandstand	1925
McArthur Court	1926
Straub Hall	1929
*10,000 square feet or more	

Aerial view of campus, 1921.

1900-1929

Gilbert Hall (formerly the Commerce Building)

The Museum of Art

ELLIS F. LAWRENCE: CAMPUS ARCHITECT

When Ellis Lawrence arrived in Portland from the East Coast in 1906, he didn't expect to stay in the city more than a few months, let alone become one of its most prominent founding architects. He was headed to San Francisco, ready to open a new office and start a new life in the West. When a massive earthquake hit San Francisco, his plans changed. Lawrence liked Portland, and decided to stay. Over the next forty years, he would leave a brilliant legacy of great buildings, thoughtful city planning and high ideals in every corner of the state—but his impact was felt in Eugene perhaps the most.

Founder of the School of Architecture and Fine Arts in 1915 (later renamed the School of Architecture and Allied Arts), Lawrence was the official campus architect from 1915 until his death in 1946. He remained a resident of Portland but traveled weekly to Eugene to work on campus. Lawrence designed dozens of buildings on campus and created a number of general campus plans—some of which were realized, some of which were not.

Through all of his projects, Lawrence held fast to high ethical and aesthetic ideals. Lawrence believed deeply in comprehensive city and campus planning, a process which didn't always fit in with the goals of real estate developers and city government. Nonetheless, Lawrence maintained his standards and produced some of Oregon's most beautiful and historic buildings, including the UO Museum of Art, the Library and dozens of other UO buildings.

He lived a well-rounded life intellectually. His mantra in architecture, "Harmony in diversity," carried over into the rest of Lawrence's world. Having studied art during his youth in the East, he often tried new media: painting, etching, even writing fiction. Lawrence wrote a number of short stories and two novels, one about a utopian community on the Oregon Coast and a mystery whose heroine was based on the UO Architecture librarian, Camilla Leach.

He designed dozens of Portland's most stately homes—many of which stand today in the hills above the city, the suburbs lining the Willamette River and the tree-lined blocks of east Portland. Lawrence's own house, which he designed in 1906, is credited with being the first Arts and Crafts style home in Oregon.

Lawrence was constantly in pursuit of larger goals, many of which centered around a public discourse about the planning and architecture of Oregon's cities. He was active in the Portland Architectural Club, serving as president in 1910. He created the Architectural League of the Pacific Coast, the Oregon Chapter of the American Institute of Architects, the Builders Exchange of Portland and the Oregon Building Congress.

—Jessica MacMurray

The Rowdy Ragtime Years

> May 8, 1923
>
> TO THE WOMEN OF THE UNIVERSITY:
>
> There are a few things to avoid, and I do not suppose you will now hear about them for the first time. But repetition may help them assume their right importance.
>
> Go picnicking in parties of four or more whenever you can. There's more fun with four, unless you are stupid in choosing your friends. Besides, you save yourself from getting involved overmuch with a man who may weary you interminably in four weeks....
>
> If you wear hiking trousers in downtown streets by necessity, don't get mentally confused and imagine you are in ordinary sports costume.... It is permissible to be conspicuous when you are beautiful—but not when you are merely comfortable.
>
> Generally, when you affront the social convictions of the great body of wholesome, middle-class people you are acting incautiously at least. Only the horribly rich and the too poor to matter can afford such a pastime.
>
> Yours,
> Grace Edgington
> Acting Dean of Women

crowds of alums and townspeople came to watch the magical spectacle; freshmen were more concerned with a bonfire into which they tossed their green caps, symbolically ending their year of bondage and qualifying them to bedevil the frosh of next year.

The nation came to realize that there was a new spirit on the campuses, brash, cheerful, rowdy; it was called jazz.

C.A. Hibbard wrote, "The student of today has given up his big red sweater and his bulldog pipe for a Fatima...and has turned from the debating society and oratorical contest to the saxophone." (The saxophone, be it noted, was regarded as the avatar of youthful degeneracy by censorious elders.)

The football team had already played in its first Rose Bowl game in 1917 when Shy Huntington quarterbacked his team to victory over Pennsylvania; now, in 1920 the Oregon team met Harvard in Pasadena.

On that pre-television, pre-radio-network day, the rooters at home could still follow the play; on the broad stage of the old Heilig Theater, a huge sheet of plywood was placed on edge, painted to represent the field, and a string-suspended football moved as telegraphic reports came in. Wild yells went up from the darkened aisles as Captain Bill Steers kicked a field goal, putting Oregon in the lead; then a deep groan as Steers was buried under a pile of burly Harvard men, knocked out of the game. Little "Skeet" Manerud, weighing only 127 pounds, went in to face the big eastern team and kicked another goal—another yell rocked the theater—but Harvard had scored and took the game 7-6.

Prince Lucien Campbell, the most popular of the University's presidents, died in 1925. In September of the next year, the University's semi-centennial was celebrated with speeches, pageants and the inauguration of President Arnold Bennett Hall on Hayward Field. That same year the big new athletic building, McArthur Court, was completed where Colonel John's cadets had practiced at war. It was used for social events as well as sports in the decades before the Student Union was built.

McArthur Court: From the Igloo to the Pit

It was the "white elephant" back in 1926. Then it was dubbed "the igloo." A 1956 brochure deemed it the "West Coast's best college basketball pavilion." Now, McArthur Court is simply known as "The Pit."

Clifton "Pat" McArthur probably never thought a place bearing his name would breed some of the most rabid and feared basketball fans in the nation. McArthur was the UO's first student body president back in 1901 and was also the first editor of the campus newspaper. He went on to serve four terms in Congress before his death in 1923.

Home first to the Webfoots, Mac Court was inaugurated with victory. The first game was held in 1927, when the UO Firs beat Willamette 38-10, and the team went on to win the NCAA championship in 1939. Today, both men's and women's basketball, along with women's volleyball and men's wrestling, shine at Mac Court. TV crews often line University Street with equipment and crews to broadcast Duck games from the venerable facility that has been called the Boston Garden of the West Coast.

But it's the fans that give the Pit its reputation. A recent poll deemed McArthur Court as Pac-10 teams' least favorite place to play. In 1995, *Sports Illustrated* listed it as one of the twelve toughest places in the country to play college basketball.

Most opposing teams still think it's a circus at the Pit. Marv Harshman, the great University of Washington coach, put Groucho Marx glasses on his team to protest fan behavior in 1976. A crowd of a little more than 9,000 paid homage to the UCLA Bruins in 1984. The new UCLA coach, Don Monson, probably wondered what he was getting into when he saw fans mobbing the court after Oregon's 62-51 upset victory. "I've had a team cut down the nets before, but never at midseason," he said.

—Dennis Fernandes

Mac Court, above, circa 1927.

Dapper Clifton "Pat" McArthur, center, 1898.

Pioneer Father: The Campus's Leading Citizen

He is especially handsome on these spring days when the sun's rays, almost cut off by Fenton's bulk, shine on him in the late afternoon. The nine-foot pioneer strides unhampered toward Johnson Hall.

When he first pushed that right foot forward on the campus, the Armistice was less than a year old. On May 12, 1919, workmen erected this first statue on campus facing south between Fenton and Friendly Halls. The sculptor, Alexander Proctor, directed the installation two years after he found his model on a ranch in Burns, Oregon. J.C. Cravens, an Eastern Oregon trapper, was discovered after a ten-year search for the type of rugged pioneer needed as a model.

The sculpture was commissioned by Joseph N. Teal, a Portland attorney, who wanted to honor the Oregon pioneer who "saved the West for this country." Teal chose the Eugene campus as the Pioneer's home to inspire Oregon youth.

After the site came the selection of the Pioneer's base. Warren D. Smith, head of the geology department, spent many days up the McKenzie searching for the right piece of basalt.

Students first saw him in this setting on commencement day, 1919. A draped American flag—once flown over the battleship *Oregon*—was released from the statue in the afternoon while 1,200 spectators watched. They listened to speeches by the donor, himself a pioneer; A.C. Dixon, vice-president of the board of regents; Herald White, student body president; R.A. Booth, twenty-five-year resident of Eugene; and Proctor.

By 1929, with the student population just short of 3,000 and the campus crowded with new buildings, the University had lost any semblance of the small-town college. No longer was it possible for students to personally know all their classmates. The young flappers and sheiks were sophisticated, worldly; the bonds that had held the "big family" together were inevitably loosening.

Coupes and roadsters complete with rumble seats whipped around the campus where, a decade ago, everyone had walked. There were even a few raccoon coats around.

Trying to enforce Prohibition, police led a few beer raids on fraternity houses; one reportedly netted "enough beer to keep Germany going for a year."

The raucous, self-confident, tradition-happy college world was preserved for posterity in a movie—written, produced, cast, directed, financed and distributed by University students in the last year of the Roaring Twenties.

Ed's Coed had its world premiere during the 1929 Homecoming, showed in a few towns around the state, then slipped into oblivion. It is occasionally revived on campus.

It is an awkward, good-natured farce-melodrama, a celebration of a brave young world that never existed—where virtue triumphs over all odds, and all goals can be reached.

Despite its timeworn cliches and its venerable plot, one can find the spirit of the old University in the film.

Here is the aged John Straub, after half a century on campus a wispy, living monument to the past, musing in a Race-side garden to the music "The Phantom Violinist." Bill Hayward, Oregon's "Grand Old Man of Track," trains another crop of athletes on the field named for him; embarrassed by the camera, he runs stubby fingers through his shock of iron-gray hair while a nervous smile creases a face like finely wrinkled brown leather. The campus of '29 is there, with the Millrace playing a major part in the plot.

Of course, the hayseed, idealistic hero and the cruel flapper heroine are reunited, and Ed is pledged into a prestigious fraternity as recompense for his comic sufferings and unselfish idealism. All ends well in the little celluloid college world. But lurking unsuspected, off camera, is a cold and sour villain—the Great Depression.

Filming Ed's Coed, *1929.*

JAMES H. GILBERT: FROM STUDENT TO DEAN

Student, professor, department head and dean, James H. Gilbert encompassed in his own life the University's transition from a provincial college to a major institution.

Graduating in 1903, Gilbert was an outstanding student with a major in economics and a strong concentration in the classics. He secured a fellowship at Columbia University, earned his Ph.D. in 1907, returned to Oregon that fall for a part-time assistantship and in 1908 became an assistant professor of economics.

He was, from the first, a remarkable teacher. He lectured "in a manner I never experienced from any other professor in my long years as a student," wrote one of his former students. "His dry, exact speech was fascinating. Instantly, he satisfied students in the one respect that students all long for and often do not get—he knew what he was talking about and he made it clear."

What he taught, he taught well. To the very last term, he was magnificent in the classroom. One of his students that year, now a University professor of economics, said of him: "He was dogmatic and he was out of date, but his teaching was impressive, vigorous, stimulating, and his class memorable."

As dean, Gilbert was efficient, decisive and unequivocal in administering the affairs of his college. He took many actions that should have endeared him to the faculty. In one case, he recommended that the Regents rescind the salary cut of a professor whose behavior had been unorthodox. At another time, he defended a professor accused of consorting with communists. His brief for that case was so succinct and decisive that it brought immediate withdrawal of the charges. He also strongly opposed and effectively lobbied against a legislator's proposal to require the faculty to sign a "loyalty" oath.

Given Gilbert's prominence, strength and influence, many have wondered why he was not named president. Some believe he was anxious for the honor; some think he was too modest to aspire to it. Many friends and former students firmly believe that he was offered the presidency and turned it down on more than one occasion.

Gilbert retired in 1947 to lecture, write and spend time with his grandchildren.

—*Robert D. Clark*

Milestones 1900–1928

1900
Sigma Nu, first fraternity, established. ASUO organized. Student newspaper renamed *Oregon Weekly*.

BUS: University catalog announces the addition of a School of Commerce.

CAS: The Department of Letters renamed the College of Literature, Science and the Arts.

MUS: The Department of Music upgraded officially to the School of Music. Wallis Gifford Nash is appointed dean.

1901
The Legislature increases the University's financial support to $47,500 per year.

1902
Prince Lucien Campbell begins his twenty-three years as fourth president. First yearbook, the *Webfoot*, published.

MUS: Wallis Gifford Nash is replaced by Irving Mackay Glen as dean.

1904
First Rhodes Scholar, Harvey Densmore, named. First sorority organized.

1908
First "O" built on Skinner's Butte.

MUS: The marching band starts under the name "Oregon Boola Band."

1909
Student newspaper renamed *Oregon Emerald*.

1910
Oregana chosen name for yearbook.

ED: School of Education established. Courses continue to be listed within CAS until 1920. Henry D. Sheldon appointed dean

1913
Plan to consolidate University with OAC defeated.

MUS: Ralph Haine Lyman appointed dean.

1914
BUS: Harry Miller asked to become the first director of the School of Commerce.

AAA: The School of Architecture and Fine Arts opens with eighteen majors.

1915
BUS: D. Walter Morton succeeds the ailing director Miller as dean.

LAW: Law School moves to Eugene from Portland.

1916
J: Journalism School established. Eric Allen, who has been the head of the journalism program since 1912, appointed dean.

MUS: "Mighty Oregon" first performed. Band director Albert Perfect organizes the Ladies Band.

ED: "Cadet" school or junior high established on campus as a laboratory school for pre-service teachers.

AAA: School of Architecture & Allied Arts
BUS: College of Business
CAS: College of Arts & Sciences
ED: College of Education
J: School of Journalism & Communication
LAW: School of Law
MUS: School of Music

1917
Military science and training added to curriculum.

MUS: John J. Landsbury appointed dean.

1918
ED: School of Education accredited by the Northwest Association of Colleges and Secondary Schools.

1919
LAW: Law school admitted to the Association of American Law Schools.

1920
Oregon Daily Emerald replaces *Oregon Emerald*. School of Physical Education established. Hayward Field opened.

BUS: Dean Morton resigns. Economics professor Edwin Clyde Robbins appointed dean. School of Commerce renamed School of Business Administration.

MUS: Oregon Marching Band moved from the School of Music to ROTC.

ED: Lab school becomes University High School, with the support of Eugene School District 4J.

1921
Authority to grant doctorate given.

AAA: The program leading to the bachelor of architecture degree is expanded to five years. Art history is listed as one of six divisions. Maude Kerns arrives to teach and lead normal arts, a position she holds until 1947.

1922
Fire destroys first gymnasium, frame building housing journalism. Phi Beta Kappa installs chapter.

AAA: Walter Ross Baums Willcox joins faculty as head of architecture. A devastating fire destroys the AAA annex including equipment, valuable plaster casts and faculty artwork.

MUS: Music building completed.

1923
AAA: The Arts Wing opens to replace the burned facilities.

BUS: Undergraduate program accredited by the American Assembly of Collegiate Schools of Business.

LAW: School accredited by the American Bar Association.

1925
President Campbell dies.

1926
Arnold Bennett Hall selected fifth president. First Ph.D. granted.

ED: School of Education begins to address needs of students with learning disabilities. Summer sessions teach special education pedagogy.

1927
AAA: The degree of bachelor of architecture in interior design offered.

1928
BUS: Dean Robbins resigns to join faculty at Harvard. David Faville appointed dean. First M.B.A. granted.

ED: School of Education Summer Clinic addresses instructional and literacy needs of students with reading difficulties. The Clinic for Exceptional Children established in the School of Education by Burchard W. DeBusk.

Until 1907 no library building existed on campus. For thirty years after the University's founding in 1876, a succession of makeshift sites, including the first floor of Collier House, were used to house the UO's modest collection of books. In 1907 the state legislature finally appropriated $25,000 for the construction of a real library. This building—now Fenton Hall, above—devoted only one floor to the library. Although electricity was available, the state funding did not include money for lighting—so for the first two years the library had to use lamps.

MUS: The School of Music becomes a member of the National Association of Schools of Music.

The Tall Firs bring glory to Eugene, 1939.

UO joins the war effort...

...but campus life moves on, 1945.

Depression, WAR AND Renaissance

The Great Depression struck the University with terrible force.

The student body dwindled, budgets were cut in half and the University might have died if certain panicky legislators had won their way. Amid the tension and anxiety of that bleak period, lighter aspects of student life were put in limbo.

The Frosh Parade, the Underclass Mix, the paddling of "tradition-violators" on the steps of Fenton Hall by burly letterman—all were dropped. Students had more serious things to consider.

The last "green lid," once a badge of freshman servitude, was presented to the freshman class president in a dignified ceremony on Hayward Field, during halftime of the first big game of the year. The class was formally welcomed by the University's president and the hazing, which had served to subordinate the frosh to the sophs, was replaced by the more solemn ritual.

Dean Karl W. Onthank, adviser to students, wrote in 1933:

> Serious disturbances in the life and activities of college students have been inevitable. Nearly all have less money. Some to whom expenses were of no consequence a year or two ago, are now faced by the stark necessity for earning their own way.... Economic distress and political and educational disturbances which have forced out of the University nearly a fifth of its normal enrollment have brought serious discomforts and anxieties to the students left in the University.

In 1929, just before the worldwide disaster, 3,536 students were enrolled; when Dean Onthank wrote his letter four years later, there were only 2,396. Onthank helped hard-pressed

by Walter Wentz

"Serious disturbances in the life and activities of college students have been inevitable. Nearly all have less money. Some to whom expenses were of no consequence a year or two ago, are now faced by the stark necessity for earning their own way...."

Depression, War and Renaissance

students to find employment, and, somehow, in a town already filled with the unemployed, work was found. "The ingenious and toilsome ways students have found to earn enough to go to college is an inspiring and sometimes pathetic story," he wrote. Legends abounded: of the fraternity man who washed dishes to pay his house bills, of the diligent student who worked most of the night to study the next day.

Emergency loans from an already tiny University fund were spread thin to cover the need, and the need was extreme. More than 10 percent of students registering that year had to have those loans just to pay their initial fees.

But youth is supremely adaptable, and the picture was not all that bleak: in a depressed economy, a good room with board might be had for $15 a month.

Social activities persisted, though drastically curtailed in expense, and "Dutch Dating" appeared. Most students no longer drove cars, of course, but campus dances increased in number and popularity. There were dances sponsored by almost every group on campus: the Military Ball, the Junior Prom, the Soph Informal, the Journalism Jam, the Senior Ball. Debating enjoyed a resurgence of popularity, though the big round-the-world tours of a few years earlier were no longer practicable.

There were some rumblings of impending danger from the state. All institutions of higher learning had been placed under control of a single state board in 1929. In 1931, the board passed a ludicrous bill containing a "suggested distribution of grades" for college students. Seven percent were to get As, and seven percent were to flunk—a bit of legislation that was sensibly ignored by college administrations.

But then came the Zorn-Macpherson Bill, which could not be ignored, for it proposed nothing less than the abolition of the University by merger with Oregon State. The bill reached the ballot by initiative petition in which the public was assured that it would "save the taxpayer's money." Then alumni, administration, students and faculty united to campaign against it.

When it came to the final vote on November 7, 1932, the bill was defeated overwhelmingly at the polls. Jubilation ensued, though the University was still in financial straits.

Faculty salaries were reduced, the professors carried on research with no remuneration beyond the costs of materials. But the upturn had begun, however slowly, and the unique flavor of University student life began to reassert itself.

Social activities persisted, though drastically curtailed in expense, and "Dutch Dating" appeared. Most students no longer drove cars, of course, but campus dances increased in number and popularity.

Arnold Bennett Hall
President 1926–1932

Arnold Bennett Hall arrived on campus in August 1926, eager to continue and even exceed the dreams of Prince Lucien Campbell. Hall was a nationally known political scientist and a Midwesterner. He had received a Doctor of Jurisprudence, cum laude, from the University of Chicago in 1907 and had taught at Chicago, Northwestern and Wisconsin. He had published four books on politics and international law and had founded the National Conference on the Science of Politics.

In his inaugural address, Hall emphasized the need for research, warning that financial parsimony could undermine the free spirit of inquiry "necessary to carry on research of the scholar." He concluded by asking friends of the University to help him continue the traditions of John Wesley Johnson and Campbell.

Hall's early optimism about the possibilities for the University soon met the stern realities of a state government committed to thrift and concerned with a tight money situation; in the 1927 legislative session, two of the five appropriation requests (the infirmary and pension plan) had to be withdrawn during committee debate. The three remaining measures (the library and budgets for Doernbecher Hospital and the Medical School) were all passed by substantial majorities in the legislature, but Governor Patterson, always a close man with the taxpayer dollar, vetoed the library bill and forced reduction in the other two. The millage rate established in 1920 did not provide sufficient funds, and the University began to lean more heavily on the Gift Campaign and the search for foundation money.

Hall brought the newest techniques in testing, advising, and counseling students and extended and emphasized the research function of a university—during a time of incredible turmoil.

This shift turned out to be one of Hall's greatest legacies to the University. He understood the importance of a strong endowment to ensure a quality institution. "... money given to the support of some form of education [is] the safest, surest, most effective way of serving the highest interests of society," he said.

Hall's book *Investments in the Future of Oregon*, written in 1930, was a trailblazer in describing the needs of the University of Oregon and ways in which donors can meet those needs. Today, there is a special society within the University's fundraising system named for Hall that recognizes donors who give to UO through a will, trust or other deferred gift.

His attention to fundraising was well timed; during his presidency, the UO faced its most intensive crisis yet. The Zorn-Macpherson Bill was introduced to voters, proposing that UO and OSU be consolidated into a single State University—headquartered in Corvallis. OSU President William Jasper Kerr led the charge, and the UO was threatened like never before or since.

It was a dramatic battle, complete with secret meetings, robberies, violent threats and disappearing petitions, but it came to an anti-climactic end. In November of 1932, the bill was defeated by a vote of almost six to one. In celebration, UO classes were dismissed the following day and Eugene merchants planned a holiday, which was followed by a dance at McArthur Court.

In the summer of 1931, Arnold Bennett Hall had suffered a heart attack, which he concealed as an attack of sciatica. This new health problem, a fine offer from the Brookings Institution, and the agreement of the State Board that he would not be considered for the chancellorship of the State System of Higher Education, induced Hall to tender his resignation and leave the state after the Zorn-Macpherson crisis was over.

The 1931 *Oregana* remembered him with reverence: "Dr. Hall, one of the foremost social scientists and educators in the nation... has attempted to advance the science of teaching, the problems of social science and to further international peace."

—*David Cunningham*

Depression, War and Renaissance

Few personalities stand out strongly in the records of the time. The hundreds of hard-working students who lived on the narrow edge of poverty in various rented rooms are seldom mentioned. The fraternities and sororities were cramped by the Depression, but the "beautiful people" of that day—Joe College, and the Sweetheart of Sigma Chi—monopolized the campus media.

When one considers that there was a huge Peace March in 1935 on the University of Oregon campus, it seems that there is truly nothing new under the sun. Hitler had been thundering his ultimatums that spring, and the worldwide horror and revulsion toward the memory of the Great War had produced a groundswell of feeling on America's campuses.

Friday, April 12, 1935, had been chosen as the day for massive nationwide demonstrations against "the method of war," and the faculty was petitioned to dismiss classes. The faculty went on record as preferring peace to war, and, without a single dissenting vote, agreed to dismiss classes from 11:00 to noon.

War protest, 1935.

A dozen campus groups organized the protest, which began with a great assembly at the steps of the old Library. More than 1,000 participants from Eugene High School, University High School, Northwest Christian College and the University listened to strangely modern-sounding speeches denouncing war profiteering, the "militarization of the campus," and the nation's unprecedented billion-dollar peacetime military budget. Then the four-block-long parade marched downtown with sound-car, banner and signs, joined by at least 500 townspeople along the way.

That same April 12 marked the revival of a controversy which had plagued the campus since 1914, the matter of compulsory military training on campus. Voting on a proposal to make ROTC optional, the faculty split evenly on the issue, forty-two to forty-two. President C. Valentine Boyer, knowing the unpopularity of his stand but feeling that military training might soon prove invaluable, cast his deciding vote for compulsory ROTC.

On the same day as the Peace March, and on those same Library steps, the grand old tradition of hacks administered by the lettermen was revived. Those who walked on lawns or the campus seal, those who smoked on campus, nonseniors wearing mustaches or sitting on the Senior Bench, freshmen neglecting to wear freshman pants, whatever those were—all were summoned to the steps by an *Emerald* announcement, called forward to take their punishment, and subjected to hacks from a paddle-wielding letterman—the number determined by severity of the offense.

Those who avoided the ordeal of bending over in public while some athlete knocked the dust from their rear elevations were pursued and subjected to double hacks or dunked in the Millrace when caught.

This conscious and enthusiastic revival of student traditions began a revamping of the old student image established in the Roaring Twenties. With a few changes, of course; the student of the Thirties was a bit more serious.

Boisterous Betas combat gloom on campus.

ERIC ALLEN: PIONEER OF UNIVERSITY JOURNALISM

Eric Allen's life story from 1912 to his death in 1944 is one of the development of a nationally recognized training school for young journalists. In those days, there were very few journalism schools in the United States. The University's journalism offices and classrooms were crowded into one small room in the basement of McClure Hall.

When Allen died, still in the midst of his work as dean, he left behind an enrollment which exceeded 300 prior to World War II, a journalism building and a University press.

The basic press equipment was given him by Harrison Kincaid, old-time publisher of the *Oregon State Journal* in Eugene. Among the equipment was the old Washington hand press which printed the first newspaper west of the Missouri, *The Oregon Spectator*.

Dean Allen was a man of varied experience in editorial, business and mechanical departments. He had tremendous enthusiasm for his work, and a gift for teaching. A wealth of nonjournalistic knowledge was evident in the dean's conversation and lectures, and he thought his students should likewise acquire more than practical professional knowledge. He made a policy of limiting a student's journalism courses to 25 percent of his or her academic load. The result was that Oregon journalism graduates had backgrounds in a wide selection of the liberal arts.

Nationally, Dean Allen was prominent. He served two terms as president of the American Association of Schools and Departments of Journalism, and a term as president of the American Association of Teachers of Journalism, an organization which he helped to establish. In 1925 he was made honorary president of Sigma Delta Chi, the national professional journalism fraternity. His articles appeared frequently in the *Journalism Quarterly* and other professional and general magazines.

Eric Allen made a permanent place for himself in the private halls of fame of innumerable journalists, students and friends. And at the University of Oregon, Dean Allen will always be remembered as a great educator and constant student.

—*Lorna Larson*

Depression, War and Renaissance

MAJOR FACILITIES AND ADDITIONS * 1929–1949	
Name	Year
Museum of Art	1930
Esslinger	1935
Volcanology	1936
Library (Fenton Hall)	1937
Chapman Hall	1939
Carson Hall	1948
Military Sciences	1948
Maintenance/Warehouses	1948
Pacific Hall	1949
Power Plant	1949
*10,000 square feet or more	

Those University holidays dedicated to the alumni—Homecoming, Junior Weekend—evolved to a point never attained before or since. Returning alumni were welcomed the night before Homecoming by a "Noise Parade" from downtown. Each living organization strove to produce more racket than any other. Huge saw blades were suspended like gongs, mounted on trailers or trucks, and hammered thunderously by crews with muffled ears. The watching public had no such protection.

By 1936, the "Swing Era" had hit the campus; Duke Ellington, Paul Whiteman and other "Big Band" stars were playing for proms and Senior Balls. The Canoe Fete had become a glittering, fantastical production that sometimes attracted nationwide attention.

The reborn school spirit finally erupted in the aftermath of the Civil War game of 1937.

On a Saturday, Oregon State beat the University, 14-0; and the next Monday, Eugene was invaded.

About 2,000 Beavers, riding as many as fifteen to a car, came down from Corvallis to indulge in a little celebration over their traditional rival's discomfiture. The caravan roared around and through the University area, the Beavers "waving cornstalks in typical Stater fashion" and shouting disparaging remarks about "duck soup." This was taken in bad part by said Ducks, who retaliated with water bags, fire hoses, tomatoes and indignant comments about "the Farm."

In the ensuing battle royal, the unfortunate Beavers, unequipped with munitions other than those being thrown at them, were routed. Campus cop Rhinesmith and Dean of Men Earl scurried ineffectually about the edges of the fracas, unable to restrain "school spirit" in the slightest. The vengeful Ducks chased the Beavers out of the campus area; Oregon State cars were stopped, the luckless passengers plucked out and dunked in the Millrace. Some foes were courteously relieved of their trousers first, so that their wallets would not be soaked during the immersion.

Some Beavers unwisely took refuge in Seymour's Cafe, from early days until its demolition a favorite haunt of youth—but the place was immediately surrounded.

The doors were hastily locked and the occupants were besieged by an army of howling, chanting Ducks.

The University was not immune to the worldwide Depression. In 1933, enrollment bottomed at 2,396, down from a 1929 high of 3,536. During the same four years, the University budget plummeted from nearly $1,500,000 to $705, 112. Faculty positions were eliminated; some were frozen and left unfilled.

The struggle against the economic realities of the Depression fell upon a faculty member named Clarence Valentine Boyer. Boyer became acting president in January 1934, president in April 1934 and was finally formally inaugurated as sixth president of the University in 1936.

He had his work cut out for him. In 1934, enrollment increased, but the budget did not increase sufficiently to handle it. Throughout the Depression, funds never quite regained the prosperous level of the pre-Depression years.

Just before Boyer took office, in an unsuccessful effort to cut costs, another radical reorganization of higher education in Oregon was proposed and actually launched. The target was duplication. No single campus was to function as a university. All science courses and their faculties were moved to Corvallis, and all social sciences came to Eugene.

Boyer had practiced law for four years after graduating from Princeton and taking his law degree at Pittsburgh. He later returned to academia, studying at Oxford, receiving a Ph.D. from Princeton and teaching at Illinois. In 1926, Boyer came to Oregon as

CLARENCE VALENTINE BOYER
PRESIDENT 1934–1938

Boyer was successful in getting new buildings on campus in the midst of the Depression. The University, using WPA and PWA money and student building fees, completed three major buildings—the Library, men's physical education building, and the infirmary—along with Howe baseball field and extensive landscaping and sidewalks.

head of the English Department. He was soon named Dean of Arts and Letters and elected to the Advisory Council.

President Boyer was involved in administrative difficulties from the start. In favor of the immediate return of science to the campus, Boyer found himself at odds with the Advisory Council, which wanted to take a slower pace in regaining these courses.

Boyer also protested the University's less-than-fair share of the available mileage tax, but with little success.

Struggles in state and local affairs presented Boyer with a divided faculty. Faculty members who had become involved politically in state affairs brought this involvement to the campus. Boyer, who disapproved of involvement in state politics, attempted unsuccessfully to focus the faculty exclusively on academic matters.

His term of office was not without its victories, however. The president was successful in getting new buildings on campus in the midst of the Depression. The University, using WPA and PWA money and student building fees, completed three major buildings—the Library, the men's physical education building and the infirmary—along with Howe baseball field and extensive landscaping and sidewalks.

In 1937, Boyer asked to resign because of ill health. The long hours and constant fights to keep the University moving forward had taken their toll. But he returned to the classroom, the deanship of Arts and Letters and the chairmanship of the Department of English and remained on the faculty until he retired in 1947. Boyer died on July 30, 1954.

—*Keith Richard*

Sports Highlights

In 1932, Laird H. Gregory of the *Oregonian*, dean of Oregon sportswriters who coined the term "Webfoots" for his alma mater, described the University as an athletically "sick" school. Basketball and baseball were both doomed to the Northern Division cellar.

The attitude of the campus was cited as the main problem; coaching was another. Howard Hobson '26 was to take care of both.

Hobby came to Eugene from Southern Oregon College in 1935. The year before, his basketball team defeated Oregon in three out of four meetings. Before going to Ashland, he had coached Benson Tech of Portland to the state high school championship.

In ten seasons at the UO, Hobson directed the baseball team to six Northern Division titles. His 169-75-3 career coaching record makes him one of the most successful coaches in UO history.

But basketball, the more visible sport, was where Howard Hobson gained national fame. He was the innovator, tactician and coaching genius of the day. His 1939 NCAA championship team is proof enough.

Hobson's first-year team at Oregon was the first twenty-game winner in school history. The lineup for an eventual national championship team was set the very next year, 1937. Quick guards Bobby Anet and Wally Johanson, who had played together under assistant coach John Warren '28 at Astoria High School, joined towering Urgel (Slim) Wintermute (6'8") and 6'4" forwards Laddie Gale and John Dick. Along the way, Gregory nicknamed them the Tall Firs.

The Tall Firs didn't become a household word until 1939. But in winning forty-four of sixty-one games you could hardly say they were sneaking up on people.

By the end of the 1939 season, Oregon had earned itself a national reputation and a place in the NCAA tournament. A reported 10,000 fans assembled in Portland to greet the team; celebrations swept the state. From then on, Hobson-coached teams broke attendance records wherever they went.

The championship meant national exposure, not only then but for years to come. Hobson became the pioneer of intersectional play, taking his teams to every part of the nation. In the early '40s, Oregon made three consecutive appearances in Madison Square Gardens, the first western school so honored.

Howard A. Hobson.

The Tall Firs, 1939.

Downtown traffic was hopelessly blocked as the bloodthirsty Ducks, some carrying hastily lettered banners denouncing the insult to Oregon prestige, swarmed around the building. City police, hopelessly outnumbered, tried vainly to persuade the mob to disperse. The crowd was cheerful, but adamant; they weren't leaving without those Staters.

So authorities entered lengthy negotiations with the trapped Beavers, who finally agreed to surrender themselves for the sake of public peace.

As the Beavers came timidly forth, they were jubilantly borne away to a rendezvous with the Millrace, and with the "O" on Skinner Butte, which needed a fresh coat of yellow paint—applied with the seats of Beavers' pants with said Beavers still in them. After this disgraceful but diverting little skirmish, relations between Oregon State and the University were more decorous for a few seasons.

In spring of 1941, the Canoe Fete was based on the theme of the "Arabian Nights." The daytime Mock Canoe Fete was titled "Stars Fell on Ali Baba," and featured floats as ludicrous as the nighttime spectacles were beautiful. That fall, heavy floods in the Willamette broke the inlet canal of the Old Millrace, and it went dry. Students worried whether repairs could be finished in time for the 1942 Fete.

Queen's Canoe, 1939.

They had more food for thought during the winter; in the *Emerald*, which was becoming more and more concerned with national and international news, they could read a debate on "Isolationism" and "Intervention" by Clinton P. Haight, and his son, student journalist William.

ISA, the Independent Students' Association, had formed to combat the Greeks' monopoly of student government. Violinist Yehudi Menuhin gave a series of newspaper interviews during a Eugene stay; the less culturally inclined might go down to the Heilig to see Frances Gifford in "Jungle Girl," or Abbott and Costello in "Keep 'Em Flying."

Donald Milton Erb
President 1938–1943

The process that made Donald Milton Erb seventh president of the University was complicated. The Advisory Council favored a choice from the existing faculty. Such a person, they argued, would be aware of recent events at the University. Wayne Morse and James H. Gilbert, both of whom had been involved in the 1933 chancellorship controversy, were among the Council's choices.

The rumor mill had correctly tabbed Donald Erb as the choice of Chancellor Frederick M. Hunter, who was ultimately charged with finding the person for the job. Hunter, with the unanimous consent of the Council, presented Erb's name to the State Board, and the members agreed.

Donald Milton Erb had been a freshman English student under former President Boyer at the University of Illinois. He had received his Ph.D. from Harvard and taught economics at the UO for four years before going to Stanford. Erb was thirty-seven years old, and it was anticipated that his youth would give the UO a president of long tenure after the short terms and lack of continuity of the past few years.

His first job was to present a budget to the Board, in the face of tight funding and burgeoning enrollment. The same problems had faced Boyer, but by now the national and state economies had recovered somewhat. Erb's budget dealt with the situation forthrightly.

Erb also continued Boyer's fight to get sciences back on campus. "Horse trading" with Oregon State, in his view, would not settle the problem. With the

Erb saw education as the foundation of the commonwealth. It was "no rare adornment for the exceptional mind, but the very fabric of the good life, conceived out of the need of a democratic people dedicated to the common good."

patience of the fine fisherman that he was, Erb never once approached the press or the public to win sympathy for his position. In 1941, after considerable persuasion and maneuvering by Erb, the State Board voted to return the University's science curricula starting with the fall term of 1942.

When World War II erupted, Erb watched the young students and faculty leave for war duty. He immediately began to make plans for the postwar University, believing the needs of the postwar student could not be met by the prewar curriculum.

One of the problems, Erb thought, would be a tremendous increase in University enrollment. He predicted that higher education would be caught off guard by a flood of returning G.I.s.

In 1943, Erb presented a proposal to the Board that would allow the University to build a student union, an idea that had originated with former President Campbell in the early 1920s. The Board accepted the proposal, and plans were initiated to finance and construct a student union.

This was Erb's last appearance before the State Board. Shortly after a return from a trip East, he caught pneumonia. By the time it was realized he had pneumonia and not the flu, the use of penicillin and sulfa drugs could not save his life. Erb died, at age forty-three, on December 23, 1943.

In 1944, acting President Orlando Hollis announced the selection of a site for the Erb Memorial Student Union; a memorial to Donald Erb and all those from the University who served and died in World War II.

In his six-year term Erb had restored the reputation of the institution and had reunited the faculty. In his 1938 inaugural address, Erb had told his audience:

"The University is under obligation to make you proud of having been a member of its student body.... The alumni can know that their assistance to their alma mater will constitute as fine an example of public service as they will ever perform. As the incoming president of the University of Oregon, I pledge myself to see that the University does its part."

He did.

—Keith Richard

Law School Dean Wayne Morse had been mysteriously absent for some days, and his housekeeper reported that his mail was being sent to the hotel in Washington D.C. where he stayed when meeting with the President or high government officials.

Exams were looming, and the dean of women announced that this weekend would be "closed"; campus women would be allowed only two dates. No entertainment at all would be allowed in the two weeks preceding exams. The late dating night was Sunday, December 7, 1941.

The *Emerald* was not published for four days. Sober essays appeared in the next issue:

In contrast with the pell-mell enthusiasm, flag waving and cheering crowds that greeted America's entry into the last war, students this week gathered in small groups and discussed the bombings, the President's messages and their own relations to it all.

Local defense authorities quietly and systematically executed a blackout. At an assembly, students were told to remain calm and continue their normal functions while coordinating every effort toward defense....

The Erb Memorial Student Union, shown soon after opening in 1950 in this aerial view, serves as a memorial to Donald Erb and as a tribute to those who served and died in World War II.

Another writer observed, "The campus is blanketed with a deathly calm, a silent seriousness. The College Side is no longer a gay gathering place for juke-playing collegians; instead they assemble there to listen to war news."

The section in the *Emerald* on Christmas gifts advised colorful oilcloth, to add a cheerful note to blacked-out windows.

Students of Japanese descent published an open letter to the *Emerald*, pledging their faith to America. The faculty called on everyone to "maintain their status quo with second and third generation Japanese on the campus," and, indeed, the students were more kindly than the national government would prove to be.

Oregon Goes to War

On December 8, 1941, 9:00 classes were cancelled so students and faculty could attend a Gerlinger Hall assembly to listen to FDR's address to Congress. At the College Side Inn that afternoon, patrons rose to their feet for a radio broadcast of the "Star Spangled Banner." In the weeks and months that followed, studying the Pacific War took precedence over upcoming finals; local bookstores quickly sold out of maps.

UO President Donald Erb convened a student assembly to summarize the situation. As much as possible, he said, business would continue as usual. Students should stay calm and refrain from spreading rumors. Men registered for the draft needed to check in at Johnson Hall, but there were no indications the ROTC program would be rushed to get them into service. Things were changing on campus and around the nation.

In January 1942, 1,000 troops on their way to Ft. Lewis, Washington, spent the night at McArthur Court, leaving just in time to clear the way for student registration. Across campus, work was underway to build a lookout on the library. Students would take turns searching the skies for any and all aircraft—even blimps, which the government had commandeered for the defense effort. The Skinner's Butte "O" was painted in camouflage. Nightly blackouts required special window coverings.

Despite publicity given to loyalty proclamations, in May the Eugene Military Mothers Service Club called the UO's Japanese-American students "serious threats." The *Emerald* strongly protested, noting that the students were "obeying regular curfew laws imposed by the military officials." As forced evacuation to military "relocation" camps proceeded town-by-town that spring, most Japanese-American students left campus.

Shortages loomed. As gas rationing approached, President Erb asked students to leave their "pleasure cars" at home. Bicycles, regarded as "somewhat of a novelty" by the *Emerald*, began appearing on campus. Coke machines disappeared from fraternities, a consequence of restrictions on sugar, bottle caps and delivery service.

Scrap drives became a familiar event. Students regularly collected rubber, copper, brass, iron, tin and other materials for manufacturing. The most poignant drive sought coins. With the 8,142 pennies presented in a Hayward Field ceremony, the University purchased a flag to honor students killed in the war. The flag would hang in Johnson Hall for the duration, bearing a growing number of gold stars, one for each student casualty.

The number of students on campus dwindled. Men classified as 4-F became the most popular dates on campus—which was primarily populated by women.

Then the Army invaded. In 1943, 243 men from the Air Corps arrived for a year of pre-meteorology courses. Another 109 pre-engineering students soon followed. By the fall, more than 900 soldiers were stamping around campus in block formation.

Although soldiers attended Saturday morning classes, they could sleep in Sundays—yet prewar curfew times limited Saturday night socializing. Seizing the moment, campus women negotiated with the administration to reschedule the Friday curfew forty-five minutes *earlier* and make Saturday curfews forty-five minutes *later*. As with everything, students adapted their world to fit the needs of a nation at war.

There were 137 stars on the Johnson Hall flag by the time the war was over.

—*Mike Lee*

Despite faculty admonitions to complete education and wait to be called on, enlistment began immediately. Then came the draft, and by spring term of 1943, huge groups of males were leaving, while men in khaki—Army and Air Corps personnel getting special training—took their places. Donald M. Erb, the friendly and likeable president who had reassured uneasy students in the first grim days, died just before Christmas, 1943. In the graduating classes, women outnumbered men by an astounding margin. Women took over what traditions were left, such as painting the "O"—but there was no Oregon football team to encourage.

At war's end, students came back with a rush. In the fall of 1946, 5,682 were admitted, double the number of 1945; the crush was inconceivable. Never before had the University had to refuse admission for lack of housing space.

More than half of those enrolling were veterans, many married; women were outnumbered on campus by two to one. "Temporary" housing sprang up in the Amazon area, Quonset huts appeared around the campus and town, trailer houses for married students were marshaled at 15th and Agate. Even venerable Villard Hall became home to some forty non-veterans. The lack of classroom space spurred a building boom.

This fat drive was one of many student drives to collect materials needed for the war effort.

A new lifestyle had come to campus: the husband took care of the cooking and the baby as he studied, while the wife worked to help support all of them.

A sort of renaissance of old traditions took place, with hackings, dunkings and so on. The Millrace was still dry from the flood of 1941, but the Fete had been transferred to rolling floats that traversed the downtown area during daylight hours. The construction of a student union—a dream eagerly discussed and encouraged by students since 1922—was finally begun in 1948. Student politics got back to the prewar pitch, with the Independent Students' Association opposing the fraternities and sororities, and mudslinging was rife during elections.

Depression, War and Renaissance

Noise parades on Willamette Street substituted for Millrace floats between 1941 and 1949.

The Millrace was set flowing again in 1949, due largely to the efforts of students. By 1950, the magnificent Erb Memorial Student Union was completed, while most of the flood of student-veterans graduated, bringing the gender balance on campus back to a more nearly equal proportion.

Enrollment settled around a sensible 5,500. The fraternities, sororities and "beautiful people" were once more in the ascendancy; the "Joe College" culture of 1935 seemed to be reborn virtually intact. With Korea, a new type of aggression had emerged to trouble the world, but University students had hardly heard of the place before. All was serene at the University of Oregon; but there were lively times ahead.

Pioneer Mother: Campus Coin Collector

When the sculptor crossed the Pioneer Mother's arms on her lap, he certainly wasn't thinking of designing an enclosure for good luck pennies. He probably never imagined that graduating seniors would toss coins into her lap, but that was the tradition for several decades after her installation. Close after the luck-seeking seniors came penny-seeking little boys of the University neighborhood. They clambered over the statue's shoulders to pocket the coins that for them brought luck in the form of penny candy.

Sculpted by Alexander Proctor, Pioneer Mother was commissioned by a vice president of the University, Burt Brown Barker, in 1927.

Not just any pioneer wife, she is modeled after Barker's mother who crossed the plains to Oregon in 1847. Although dedicated to all the unsung heroics of the pioneer mothers, she doesn't depict the struggle and hardship characteristic of the Oregon Trail trip. Barker wanted a statue of the woman in the "sunset of her life, drinking in the beauty and peace of the afterglow of her twilight days."

Her site was not chosen until a cardboard facsimile of the statue was placed at various positions on the campus. In the center of the women's quadrangle, the Mother was placed close enough to several paths to catch bits of University chatter.

She came to the quad on May 10, 1932, stealing the Junior Weekend spotlight from a campus queen. Barbara Barker, daughter of the donor, unveiled the $30,000 bronze lady. A letter from President Herbert Hoover was read commending Burt Barker for his gift to the University.

Harry K. Newburn
President 1945–1953

When Harry Kenneth Newburn became the eighth UO president in 1945, he faced major problems. Under the GI Bill, great numbers of young men and women were attending college who would never have done so before the war. The campus was under-staffed and under-built. Classroom space was inadequate. Dormitory space was at a premium and married student housing did not exist to any extent.

Newburn inherited these problems and gave their solutions a solid start. Originally from Illinois, Newburn was educated at Western Illinois Teachers College and received a Ph.D. from the University of Iowa. More importantly, while he was in Iowa, he became a teacher. He was appointed dean of the College of Liberal Arts at Iowa, and came to Oregon from there.

From the time of his appointment in late 1944 until his assumption of office on July 1, 1945, Newburn remained in constant communication with Acting President Orlando Hollis and Chancellor Frederick Hunter. The University faced many problems—and Newburn knew it.

Of everything, the influx of students in Eugene was Newburn's biggest challenge. In 1945 the enrollment had been 1,880 and by January 1946 it was 3,396—an 81 percent increase. Of this number, 1,192 were veterans. Spring term of 1946 saw an enrollment of 3,409. The numbers continued to grow until the downturn of 1950. Newburn had a huge student body with new needs and new experiences to accommodate.

The influx of students in Eugene was Newburn's biggest challenge. In 1945 the enrollment was 1,880 and by January 1946 it was 3,396—an 81 percent increase.

While the student body grew, the faculty ranks were reduced. Many faculty members on campus since the Campbell administration were retired by 1947. The experienced faculty was winnowed, and Newburn and the deans had to replenish it in a highly competitive market. Oregon was at a particular disadvantage since faculty pay scales had been stable since the 1930s and were among the lowest in the nation. Newburn had to—and did—convince the legislature to increase salaries.

The immediate demand for housing was met by temporary buildings. Four projects were built for married students, and single students were housed in Veterans' Dormitories on Alder Street and near the Music School. Classes were held in Quonset huts, and Emerald Hall provided needed administrative space.

Newburn's tenure saw other kinds of controversy. One of the most volatile issues was a product of the McCarthy era: the loyalty oath for faculty members. Opposition to the oath generated hot debate both on and off campus. The oath was finally watered down to acceptable strength, and the issue faded away.

The most lasting controversy of the Newburn era was the decision to sell the Miner Building to Eugene Medical Center, Inc. The building was a 1933 gift to the University from Wilber E. and Henry T. Miner. In late 1946, Newburn approached a group of doctors about purchase of the building. The sale was made, with Board approval, in May of 1947, and the University received $355,000 for the building and adjacent parking lot. Today it is felt by many that the University would have profited more by keeping the downtown building.

The Newburn tenure included some other important milestones, among them the replacement of the old Alumni Holding Company with the Development Fund in the late 1940s. The number of graduate degrees also increased dramatically during the latter part of his administration.

In June 1953, Newburn accepted a position as head of a new Ford Foundation Center for Educational Television and Radio. He went on to be named president of the University of Montana and Arizona State. Harry Newburn passed away in 1974.

—Keith Richard

Milestones 1929–1950

1929
AAA: Andrew Vincent (drawing and painting) joins the fine arts faculty, a position which he holds for forty years.

MUS: Marching band performs first halftime show at a football game.

1930
"Mighty Oregon" becomes a nationwide hit after Fred Waring and the Pennsylvanians play the tune for the Carnation Contented Hour radio show.

1931
AAA: Brownell Frasier joins faculty, soon becomes interior design program director, a position she holds until her retirement in 1966.

1932
President Hall resigns. W.J. Kerr made chancellor and head of University and Oregon State. Zorn-Macpherson Bill to combine institutions at Corvallis defeated. Science courses moved to Corvallis.

AAA: The State Board of Higher Education moves fine arts and landscape architecture to the UO from Corvallis. Fred Cuthbert is first full-time faculty member.

BUS: Dean Faville resigns. Oregon State Board of Higher Education appoints Harrison Val Hoyt interinstitutional dean and director of business administration for all of the state schools.

CAS: The College is separated into the College of Arts and Letters and the College of Social Science.

ED: James R. Jewell appointed dean.

1934
C. Valentine Boyer named sixth president. William Parry Murphy '14 awarded Nobel Prize.

BUS: The School begins offering M.S. and M.A. degrees, in addition to the M.B.A.

LAW: Order of the Coif is installed.

1936
BUS: Economics professor Victor Pierpont Morris appointed dean.

1937
ED: The Clinic for Exceptional Children renamed the DeBusk Memorial Clinic for Exceptional Children.

1938
Donald M. Erb named seventh president.

1939
Oregon wins first NCAA Basketball Championship 46-33.

MUS: Theodore Kratt appointed dean.

1941
LAW: Orlando Hollis becomes acting dean as Dean Wayne Morse's remains in Washington D.C. as a national labor arbitrator.

1942
Army, Air Force training units stationed on campus.

CAS: The College of Arts and Letters is again combined with the College of Social Science and renamed the College of Liberal Arts.

1944
J: Eric Allen, first dean of Journalism, dies while planting trees. Professor George Turnbull is named acting dean and assumes the role permanently in 1945.

1945
Harry K. Newburn named eighth president. Portland Dental School joins University.

LAW: Dean Wayne Morse resigns deanship to run for U.S. Senate. Orlando Hollis named School of Law Dean.

1946
AAA: Ellis Lawrence dies in his room in Collier House. Sidney W. Little is appointed dean.

BUS: Catherine Jones, the first female administrator in the School, joins the faculty.

1947
Athletic Director Leo Harris, third from left above, strikes a handshake agreement with Walt Disney, far right, to use Donald Duck as the official University mascot.

AAA: Marion Dean Ross arrives to teach history of architecture.

ED: Paul Jacobson appointed dean.

1948
J: Dean George Turnbull retires. Clifford Weigle appointed dean.

AAA: School of Architecture & Allied Arts
BUS: College of Business
CAS: College of Arts & Sciences
ED: College of Education
J: School of Journalism & Communication
LAW: School of Law
MUS: School of Music

IN THE STACKS: THE UNIVERSITY LIBRARY

In 1937, the grand Lombardic-style building at the corner of 15th and Kincaid became the University Library's permanent home. With its French and Italian marble, wrought iron gates and ornamented doors, the library now houses the second largestcollection of books in the Pacific Northwest and is the only research library in Oregon that belongs to the Association of Research Libraries. Its construction provided the campus with its first modern and efficient library and marked an important step in the UO's evolution as a major university.

In 1908, President Prince Campbell hired the UO's first professional librarian for the library in Fenton Hall. Matthew Douglass, from Grinnell College in Iowa, was committed to making the library as professional and efficient as those he was accustomed to in the Midwest.

In the same year, funds were made available to bring electricity into the building and more space was given over to library use. For the first time the hours were extended into the evening. What had been a book budget of $400 to $1,000 per year now was $5,000 and rising. It did not take long for the

library to expand into all of the available space in the building.

Between 1908 and 1928 the library collection grew from 16,000 volumes to 193,000. Floor space more than quadrupled and was split between several locations. Enrollment at the UO, meanwhile, shot up from 304 to 3,136.

Then came the Depression. A drop in enrollment in the early 1930s helped alleviate the overcrowding, but it also meant a slashed budget, smaller salaries and a shrunken library staff.

The New Deal brought some needed help. Federal money became available to pay student workers, making it possible for more students to attend the University and providing some staff to do routine tasks in the library.

But to Douglass, the New Deal meant federal dollars to construct a new library through the Public Works Administration. He and architect Ellis Lawrence put together detailed plans for a new building—they had done some twenty-five plans since 1921—and submitted them to the State Board of Higher Education and then to Washington, where they were rejected.

But Douglass was not going to give up. He contacted Oregon U.S. Senator Fred Steiwer to have him help prepare the way for a second request. The senator worked hard, and soon after Douglass sent in the second request, it was approved.

The UO got an outright gift of $131,000, a loan of $217,000 and a grant of $98,000. Gifts from alumni and friends of the Library added another $14,047. Including furnishings, the cost of the new Library was $460,047.80—and no state funds were expended in this construction.

On May 3, 1937, at 7:45 A.M. the new Library opened. Additions in 1950 and 1966 made room for over 1 million books and allowed 2,700 readers to use the facilities at once.

The 1994 addition brought yet another new era to the Library's story. The $25 million renovation added new space to the crowded building, and incorporated award-winning energy efficiency and accommodations for technological updates. As always, the future means growth. But the growth of the Library means that the UO is healthy, active and vital.

—Keith Richard

Excavation begins, and the completed east entrance, top.

Dunking at the freshman fountain.

A geodesic dome was built as an architecture project, 1953.

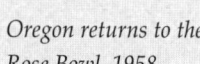

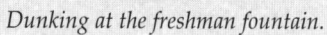

Oregon returns to the Rose Bowl, 1958.

Ducks celebrate their official mascot status.

Fifties, meet the Sixties
Sweethearts and Sit-ins

by John Thomas

In 1950 Harry Truman sent troops to Korea to stop the communists. Senator Joseph McCarthy was charging that communists had infiltrated the State Department. The State Department voted to help France finance its war against something called the Viet Minh in an obscure Southeast Asian country.

But the university students of the '50s, a University of Pennsylvania study later concluded, were "gloriously contented" with their lot, which included bright prospects, few worries and ample material rewards. Career-oriented students were eager to get their share and competed sharply with one another to get it. Ethics were your own business, mostly, and world issues were something that had little bearing on most. The study called it the "silent" or "sure thing, safe bet" generation.

"…No one seems to care about anything," said a student in an *Oregon Daily Emerald* poll. "Frankly, I'm worried about our apathy and our conformity."

"What happens when our happy little world falls 'round our ears?" wondered Bill Cook '58 in a later *ODE* editorial.

On the surface, at least, there seemed to be a superficial approach to life and the world in '50s collegiate life. There was a kind of open season on dunking. You could get thrown into the Millrace or Fenton Hall pool for almost anything, it seemed: walking on the grass, not wearing a beanie, stepping on the Oregon Seal, not saying hello or being elected King of Hearts at the Heart Hop.

And there were bonfires, the Whiskerino (which was about the only place you saw beards in those days) and painting the

…high school students interviewed in the Oregon Daily Emerald *seemed to see the University as a kind of adult playground. The University was moving from knickers to long pants, and other events of the period proved it.*

"O" up on Skinner Butte—you used a bucket of yellow paint and spread it with a handy backside.

The Beautiful People—the ones who caught the eyes and headlines of the media—seemed to be concerned with fashion and beauty contests. In 1950, Barbara Calvert was elected Miss Vogue and Mary Margaret Jones and Phyllis Morgan became co-queens for Junior Weekend in a tie vote. By the end of the decade, there were other competitions, other titles and more publicity: the *Oregon Daily Emerald* Cover Girl, the Sweetheart of Sigma Chi, Dream Girl of Pi Kappa Alpha, Moonlight Girl of Phi Sigma Kappa, Little Colonel, Homecoming Queen and a dozen other Maids, Queens, Darlings and Sweethearts.

The Millrace banks attracted bathing beauties all through the 1950s.

Oregon State students caught on campus could expect almost anything. Males sometimes had an "O" cut into their hair and were forced to wash the windows of the Student Union or polish the Oregon Seal. Once, in retaliation for the theft of the "O," University students kidnapped the Oregon State Homecoming Queen and princesses. They were photographed wearing University letterman sweaters and then released. After that, the Oregon Homecoming court went around with a burly bodyguard to prevent another retaliation.

Campus humor was sometimes clumsy and insensitive by today's standards. In 1951, Duck Preview featured a variety show—"The All Campus Vodvill." One highlight was Delta Upsilon's "minstrel show" featuring a number of the fraternity brothers in blackface delivering what was described as "sparkling repartee" to some 600 high school students and guests.

Duck Preview was discontinued in 1957, partially as an attempt to escape the "country club" label the University had been stuck with since the late '40s. High school administrators and parents were criticizing the heavy emphasis on social activities, and high school students interviewed in the *Oregon Daily Emerald* seemed to see the University as a kind of adult playground. The University was moving from knickers to long pants, and other events of the period proved it.

On Homecoming weekend in 1954, 200 freshman women had marched and demonstrated near campus, loudly booing the Order of the O, a chief enforcer of University traditions and the principal dunker of violators, real or imagined. Two women deliberately walked on the grass and the Oregon Seal, flouting those traditions and the fact that violators had been branded with a red mark on their foreheads earlier that day.

The traditionalists later retaliated by waterhosing nearly fifty women in front of the Sigma Chi house.

How to get into college

—from *Old Oregon*, August 1952

About the middle of September 1952, Barry Hugh Briggs, seventeen years old, graduate of Cleveland High School in his hometown of Portland, will come rolling into Eugene to join about a thousand other young people for the University of Oregon's seventy-sixth freshman week.

Freshmen may feel that no one gave thought to their arrival, but actually a lot of planning will have already been done. Frosh week is a reasonably orderly procedure, although to Barry and the others it may be confusing and hectic. He'll write his name at least a hundred times, it will seem. He'll take five to eight hours of examinations. He'll meet dozens of new people—faculty, dormitory advisers, roommates, maybe even President Newburn. He'll pose for a picture, breathe deeply for a physical examination, and ponder the finely printed schedule of classes. At the end of seven days of going and coming, standing in line, filling out forms and hunting up places like Villard and the new Commonwealth building, he will be a full-fledged University of Oregon student.

"Any Oregon high school graduate is eligible for admission to the University," explains the director of admissions, Spencer Carlson '35. The philosophy, he continues, is that, "as a public institution, the University should extend the opportunity to every Oregon high school graduate to demonstrate his ability to do college work."

Two out of every three high school students whose admission requests are granted actually come to the University, Carlson reports. As each student is accepted, he receives a notice of admission well in advance of September 14.

Along with this slip, the potential Webfoot gets a catalog and a little pamphlet that includes a map of the campus. The welcome pamphlet gives an idea of the fast pace which Barry will keep that week. Dormitories open on the first day. Registration material is ready the second.

An important part of the material will be a stack of IBM cards. All registration records are now kept on the intricate machines. This process was put into effect over several years and was completed in 1951.

Starting Monday, and continuing through the week, Barry and his classmates will go through their placement examinations. the basic test is the "psych" examination. This is an old standby of freshman week, having been part of the procedure since 1926. Results of this test are added to the registration materials, and a score of 5 to 9 indicates that the student has a good chance of success in college work.

There are plenty of other tests. English, mathematics and language examinations determine which courses a student is ready to take and help faculty advisors guide the students in selecting classes.

Freshman week isn't all official doings. There are informal events like the new student picnic, the traditional football rally, the student union open house and the Hello Dance, which provide some of the color and excitement of college life.

In the words of the welcome pamphlet: "So you are welcomed, examined, oriented, advised, registered—you are ready for your real University work to begin…. We wish you success!"

Sweethearts and Sit-ins

STATION KWAX ON THE AIR

The words of Dick Hardie, KWAX station manager, opened the first broadcast of the University's radio station in April of 1951. The long struggle for establishment of a campus radio station dates back to 1922 when a few experimental broadcasts were aired over a "high-power transmitting set" owned by a University student.

Not until 1949 did University radio receive real encouragement. That year, modern studios were completed on the third floor of Villard Hall and a small campus station, KDUK, made a brief appearance.

In the fall of 1950, applications were made to the Federal Communications Commission for construction and licensing of a ten-watt FM noncommercial station. The license was granted in May of 1951 and the UO's broadcast dreams finally went live.

In 1957, a group of women emerged dripping and indignant from an improvised dunking tank operated by the Order of the O. The women demanded—and got—payment for cleaning and replacement of ruined clothing. The expense curtailed a certain amount of dunking in the future, although it did not discourage it altogether.

Two years later, there was a quiet crackdown on campus hi-jinks following a number of complaints to Golda Wickham, then dean of women. Kappa Kappa Gamma was on social probation for unspecified reasons having to do with "conduct of their winter term house dance." Some high school students, visiting the Alpha Tau Omega house, had been jailed for illegal possession of alcohol.

An enduring critic of the Greek *dolce vita*, the *Emerald* reported "...limp co-eds in formal attire hanging on to car doors while losing their over-indulged liquor...loudspeakers booming music over the whole neighborhood...cars abandoned on front lawns...blocking streets...."

"These incidents—and others more racy—have not been uncommon," the *Emerald* concluded smugly.

Not everyone participated in the gay, mad social whirl of the sororities and fraternities, or even wanted to. In 1958, there were 6,000 students on campus—1,000 of whom were veterans back from Korea and 1,500 of whom were married. The Greeks represented only about one-third of the enrolled students. "It is refreshing to note that 3,000 members of the 'country club set' support themselves, in part or entirely...," observed Associate Professor W.A. Dahlberg of the speech department.

Still others maintained that students were about the same as they had always been—no more or less serious than ever. Headlined parties and social events, they maintained, were given distorted emphasis.

"Students play chess, discuss Kafka, read poetry aloud and listen to classical music with the same frequency and ease we display in attending rallies or electing queens," insisted Barbara Burns '59.

The first 2,100 war babies enrolled as freshmen in the fall of 1959. Because of the live-in rule that persisted into the '60s, they spent their first year on campus in one of the dorms. More than 300 of them met Mildred McMahon, who prepared for her ninth year as house mother at Carson Hall. The first year was always the hardest on University women, she said.

violation would result in the closure of the offending chapter. Most campus leaders thought the decision fair.

It was the year the Co-op Board made known its plans to tear down the old Willcox Building—The College Side Inn, or simply the Side—after thirty-nine years of faithful service. Vic Sabin, an architecture student, would rally a majority of students to "Save The Side," but the Co-op Board would ignore them. The following summer, after a stockholders' vote of 362 to 354 to tear it down, The Side would become a parking lot and then a new Co-op.

By the time Homecoming drew near, the traditionalists were extremely uneasy. The year before had been very hard on such things as the Sophomore Whiskerino, the Mortar Board Ball, Mystic Sales and the Bunyon Derby. Three students, Chuck Aylsworth, Ruth Zemeck and Paul Seymour, had staged a small sit-in on the Oregon Seal. "If people have to be prevented from walking on the Seal, then it's obvious that keeping off the Seal is no longer a tradition," said Seymour.

Other things were becoming more important. The assassination of John F. Kennedy overshadowed Homecoming, as University students were coming back from voter registration drives in Mississippi with new ideas about their country.

There were still collegiate-style traditions and pranks. Law students were still spending "Lawst" weekend in painters' caps looking for a queen. Students were stomping and surfing in the Bottom of the Bowl. A Saint Bernard from Phi Kappa Psi entered in a campus beauty contest was disqualified on an academic technicality (not enough credit hours). And, in 1965, while some students responded to antiwar movements, VISTA and SCOPE, others attended an "Ugly Man" contest or watched Donkey Basketball.

But more was being said about a new breed of students, who were more socially conscious than their predecessors, and more writers and speakers were referring to a growing restlessness on the nation's campuses. Educational conferences began to include scare speeches about what was to come.

"Most students have found college and education unrelated to the social realities of the time," observed Phil Sherburne '64, then president of the National Student Association. "The experiences of students in CORE, SNCC and, of course, the Peace Corps have led to a disenchantment with education."

U.S. Communist Party leader Gus Hall drew an audience of 10,000 to Hayward Field in February 1962.

Milestones 1950–1975

1950
Freshman live-in rule established.

J: The FCC authorizes a campus radio station, KDUK. Dean Clifford Weigle leaves to become associate director, then dean of Stanford's journalism school. Gordon Sabine named dean.

1953
President Newburn resigns.

AAA: R. Buckminster Fuller visits. A thirty-six foot geodesic dome is built east of Lawrence Hall. Dean Little appoints Wallace Baldinger director of the Museum of Art.

ED: University High ceases as the laboratory school for preparing teaching, as UO makes partnership agreements with a variety of local schools.

1954
O. Meredith Wilson named ninth president.

1955
J: Dean Gordon Sabine resigns to head the School of Journalism at Michigan State University. Charles Duncan named acting dean, then appointed dean the following year.

LAW: Professor Kenneth O'Connell is appointed to the Oregon Supreme Court; later he becomes Chief Justice.

1956
Jim Bailey runs first sub-four-minute mile on American soil while competing for Oregon. Walter Brattain M.A. '26 awarded Nobel Prize. Distinguished Service Award created.

MUS: The School of Music begins the International Center for Music Education, a series of ten year-long programs in Germany and England.

1957
Development Fund incorporated. The first Ersted Award for teaching is given to law professor Charles Howard.

AAA: Jan Zach arrives to teach sculpture. He retires in 1979, the same year the Museum of Art presents a retrospective exhibition of his work.

BUS: Longtime dean Victor Pierpont Morris resigns.

1958
AAA: Portland architect Walter Gordon becomes dean and emphasizes the importance of studying architectural history and broader liberal education for architects.

BUS: Dean Richard Wadsworth Lindholm appointed. Norman Taylor organizes the Forest Industries Management Center.

1959
Honors College formed.

1960
President Wilson resigns.

1961
Arthur Flemming named tenth president.

AAA: Walter Gordon resigns. Marion Ross serves as acting dean.

1962
Oregon wins NCAA Track Championship. Free Speech Platform created. Virgil Boekelheide first faculty member named to National Academy of Science.

BUS: Graduate program is accredited in 1962 by the American Assembly of Collegiate Schools of Business.

J: Dean Charles Duncan leaves to become dean at the University of Colorado at Boulder. John Hulteng appointed dean.

1963
AAA: Walter Creese begins term as dean. Marion Dean Ross begins fifteen-year period as head of art history. Official departmentalization of the school occurs: architecture, landscape architecture and urban planning, fine arts, art history and art education.

MUS: Robert M. Trotter appointed dean.

1964
AAA: Ph.D. in art education established with College of Education and later is solely administered by art education. June King McFee establishes the Institute for Community Art Studies. Gordon Kensler and McFee serve as directors.

1965
Library collection passes 1,000,000 volumes.

BUS: First European Exchange Program in Business Administration group goes to the Netherlands.

1966
AAA: LaVerne Krause (painting and printmaking) joins the faculty after teaching in Portland. She is credited with building the printmaking program into a flourishing major offering a masters of fine arts.

1967
AAA: Fred Cuthbert serves as acting dean and then dean.

BUS: School of Business Administration renamed the College of Business Administration and reorganized into two schools: the Undergraduate School of Business and the Graduate School of Management.

J: Columbia Scholastic Press Association established through gift of Lila A. Wallace.

LAW: Orlando Hollis steps down as dean. Plans begin for new building.

1968
President Flemming resigns.

AAA: The first listing of a five-year curriculum leading to the degree of the bachelor of fine arts appears in the University catalog.

LAW: Ocean and Coastal Law Center established. Law Librarian Lois Baker retires after thirty years. Gene Scoles is appointed dean.

1969
Acting President Charles Johnson killed in auto accident. Robert Clark named eleventh president. University elected to Association of American Universities. *Oregana* stops publication.

LAW: Board of Visitors started.

MUS: Marching Band cancelled due to budget cuts and protests over militaristic nature.

1970
Esslinger Hall, ROTC building damaged by fire. Bomb explodes in Johnson Hall. First cross-country NCAA championship won.

AAA: Urban and regional planning becomes a separate department.

MUS: Oregon Bach Festival begins as a two-day workshop.

ED: Robert Gilberts appointed dean.

1971
Johnson Hall sit-in, sixty-three students arrested. Basement of Prince Lucien Campbell Hall bombed.

AAA: Robert Harris becomes dean of the school.

BUS: Dean Lindholm resigns to devote more time to teaching and writing.

MUS: Marching Band revived.

1972
Steve "Pre" Prefontaine runs at the UO and solidifies Eugene's status as Track Town, USA.

BUS: Richard West appointed dean.

LAW: Law school switches to semester system.

MUS: The nationally renowned Jürgen Ahrend organ is completed, thanks to a bequest by Robert Vinton Beall.

1973
University negotiates official contract with Walt Disney Productions for use of Donald Duck's image.

LAW: Dean Scoles resigns.

MUS: Beall Hall named.

1974
LAW: Orlando Hollis retires from active teaching.

1975
Robert Clark becomes first president to retire from University. William B. Boyd named twelfth president. *Oregana* revived.

LAW: Chapin Clark begins tenure as dean. Associate Professor Dave Frohnmayer is elected to state legislature.

J: Dean Crawford resigns. John Hulteng returns to serve a second term as dean.

MUS: Morette L. Rider appointed dean.

AAA: School of Architecture & Allied Arts
BUS: College of Business
CAS: College of Arts & Sciences
ED: College of Education
J: School of Journalism & Communication
LAW: School of Law
MUS: School of Music

Major Facilities and Additions * 1950–1974	
Name	Year
Student Union (EMU)	1950
Library addition	1950
Earl Complex	1954
Walton South	1958
Walton North	1959
Westmoreland Housing	1960
Leighton Pool	1960
Columbia Hall	1960
Onyx Bridge	1960
Hamilton Complex	1961
Prince Lucien Campbell Hall	1962
Bean Complex	1962
Student Health Facility	1965
Library addition	1966
Autzen Stadium	1967
Klamath Hall	1967
Computing Center	1967
Lawrence addition	1968
Law School (McKenzie Hall)	1969
Gerlinger Annex	1969
Huestis Hall	1973
Oregon Hall	1974

*10,000 square feet or more

By 1966, returning Peace Corps and VISTA volunteers began to notice distinct but still limited changes in student lifestyles. More Oregon students were living together rather than getting married. Timothy Leary had been on campus, but his presence actually did little more than spotlight what was already happening by that time.

Marijuana had begun to replace alcohol as a social drug in some discreet social circles. *Emerald* editor Annette Buchanan's story on the situation attracted a great deal of attention from local law enforcement officers alarmed by the degree to which marijuana use had already spread. Buchanan paid a $300 fine, however, rather than reveal the sources of her information to a Lane County grand jury and District Attorney William Frye.

Frye, himself a University School of Journalism graduate, called Buchanan a "publicity hunting little snip" and a "smart-aleck kid."

Actual membership in political action groups was still small—almost equally divided between the leftist Students for a Democratic Society (SDS) and the conservative Young Americans for Freedom.

The largest group was in the middle—students vaguely concerned with the larger issues, but mainly bewildered or irritated by local campus groups and hurrying by the leafleteers who grew in numbers outside Erb Memorial Student Union.

All campus groups began to feel the changing times—not least of which were the Greeks.

In 1967, Tom Trovato—president of Alpha Tau Omega—urged the campus to "lean on the hippies," whom he maintained were more of a threat to the student body than anyone realized.

What had distressed the ATOs was a "chalk-in" involving a small group of sidewalk artists who decorated the EMU terrace with floral geometric designs. The ATOs, claiming the designs had obscene and antiwar significance, roughed up two of the artists—Brandy and Lee Feldman, both prominent in SDS activities.

Campus reaction, however, was sharply critical of the "demented" and "pathetic attempts" to prove masculinity. Another letter compared the behavior to Jew baiting in the '30s, while another said that chalk was much preferable to the paint used by many of the fraternities on house sidewalks.

A year later, Theta Chi pledged Larry Holliday, a black basketball star from Los Angeles. "Why make a big issue of it?"

1950–1975

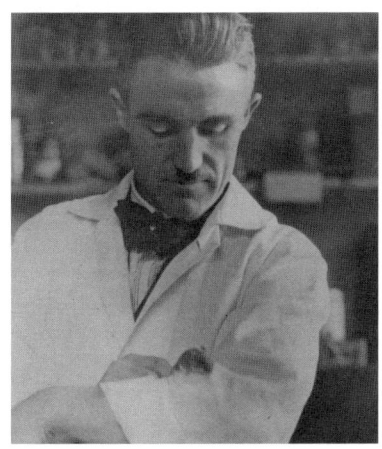

RALPH HUESTIS: OF MICE AND A MAN

For more than forty years, Ralph Huestis conducted research on the genetics of a species of mouse called *Peromyscus paniculatus*, the deer mouse. During this period, Huestis had more than 40,000 subjects for his research. He usually had on hand about 1,500 mice at a time, many of which he and his assistants had trapped on excursions to the Oregon Coast, in Eastern Oregon or just out in a field in Eugene. They brought the trapped mice back to Huestis's lab, appropriately called the Mouse House, to begin examining the mice for mutations.

Wild deer mice are common in most parts of North America, and their ancestors have neatly adapted to their local environments, taking on the size, proportions and behavior most likely to keep the species alive and healthy. Geneticists like Huestis believe that this refinement of structure and function has been brought about by continuous random alterations of the genetic information passed from generation to generation.

And while the layperson may find pure, disinterested research and classification uninteresting, Huestis never ceased to be most impressed with the spectacular discovery that had immediate meaning in his own lifetime. Sometimes these discoveries are simply happy accidents—as when Professor Huestis found among his colony *Peromyscus* that carried spherocytosis.

When Huestis and his assistant, Ruth Willoughby (now Dr. Ruth Willoughby Anderson), discovered that one in three of the *Peromyscus* colony carried one gene for the disease, they knew they had something pretty important. The pair went on to test and selectively breed the spherocytic mice before calling on the aid of Dr. Arno Motulsky, a hematologist from the University of Washington.

Thus began a long, trial-filled investigation and series of experiments with the transfer of bone marrow tissue from healthy mice into very young, diseased offspring. If the healthy tissue would adapt, perhaps the unhealthy tissue would not develop. Such proved to be the case after many unsuccessful attempts and the final results were satisfying indeed.

Theoretically, such a cure could be effected on the offspring of human beings whose genetic structure passed spherocytosis or other hemalytic disease to their young. "It's the same kind of thing they're trying to do with cancer victims today," said Huestis.

The scientist was self-effacing about his role in the research on the spherocytic mice, just as he was when he appraised his many years of work in the Mouse House. "Present a moron with an insoluble problem," he said with a smile, "and he'll stick with it forever."

Huestis Hall opened in 1973.
—*Robert Larue*

---

asked Holliday, the fourth black man to join a fraternity in University history. The event was hailed as a "quiet kind of social progress" by the press. At that time, only one black woman had ever even signed up for rush in the entire sixty-year history of University sororities. Edwina Hill '66 had withdrawn, shortly after signing up, never actually participating in the 1962 rush.

With an eye toward opening up pledging, the Inter-Fraternity Council endorsed a reform measure to do away with "gentlemen's agreements" not to pledge racial minorities. Later, mysteriously, the IFC withdrew its endorsement.

"The alumni got to us," admitted one fraternity president.

Arthur S. Flemming
President 1961–1968

In February 1961 the State Board of Higher Education anounced that the tenth president of the University would be Arthur Sherwood Flemming.

Arthur Flemming had been appointed Secretary of Health, Education and Welfare in the Eisenhower cabinet in 1958. He came to UO with vast experience, and his knowledge of government enabled the institution to extend its funding through federal grants. It was an opportunity that allowed for fuller development during the '60s, but also for financial setbacks when federal money was no longer available.

University enrollment, especially in the Graduate School, increased during the Flemming administration. Faculty size and curriculum were expanded. The School of Librarianship, established in 1966, was the first new professional school on campus since 1920. The School of Community Service and Public Affairs was established with one of the largest gifts ever made to the University—more than $1.5 million from Lila Acheson Wallace '17.

Flemming urged the development of a Peace Corps training center on campus and was elated when many UO students signed up. He was similarly instrumental in the U.S. Government-University contract to open a Job Corps Center at Tongue Point.

His administration was open to students and he cooperated in the development of student-created programs. At times, as had President Campbell, he used his personal funds to assist students.

His dedication and involvement were balanced by a fair

> *Flemming felt that the campus must be free of pressure from without so that new ideas —even those he rejected personally— could flow freely within.*

amount of controversy. Flemming was outspoken and "larger-than-life"—qualities that did not always endear him to the campus community or the citizens of Oregon.

His presidency had more than its share of scandal. When, in 1962, Flemming allowed U.S. Communist party secretary Gus Hall to speak on campus, right-wing factions waged an enormous campaign to prevent the speech. A few years later, the political storm Flemming had started with the Hall speech blew up again. A series of dramatic conflicts erupted over so-called dirty poems in the *Northwest Review*, a racy movie shown in the student union and a sex scandal involving an underage young woman and a number of male UO students.

Flemming defended the students' right to invite controversial speakers to campus, and the UO literary quarterly's right to publish material that detractors considered obscene. He felt that the campus must be free of pressure from without so that new ideas—even those he rejected personally—could flow freely within.

Flemming's critics were vocal, and the controversies intensified as the years passed. Toward the end of his time at UO, complaints that the University was falling apart turned into aggressive letter-writing campaigns calling for his dismissal. The complaints centered around rampant drug use on campus, racial tension and a laissez-faire administrative policy. Flemming knew that his time was limited.

Student leaders rallied around him, staging sit-ins and posting signs in support of the controversial president. For them, he was the voice of forward thinking and a warrior against the establishment. Unfortunately, the gap between angry Oregonians and young UO students was vast.

In 1968, Flemming was faced with a decision: Macalester offered him a presidency with a clean slate, a large endowment and without mandatory retirement. Oregon had strict retirement rules, very little money and a huge amount of controversy. Flemming resigned, but the controversies continued. Charles Johnson, the incoming acting president, said himself that he had to fill "a mighty large pair of shoes" left by Arthur Flemming.

—*Keith Richard*

From 1965 to 1969, the number and frequency of rallies and demonstrations grew. They were mostly contained and peaceful, with few incidents. An April 1968 sleep-in at Johnson Hall won equal student representation on the committee that picked Flemming's successor. Charles Johnson, whom most University people remembered as a man with a strong business background, was named acting president for the interim.

Johnson's time on campus, although he was popular with both conservative and liberal students, was extremely difficult. Black Panthers drilled on campus, sororities and fraternities were closing down for lack of pledges. Activists erected wooden shacks on the EMU lawn and proposed to live in them to show poverty to the University. An SDS leaflet showing a symbolic

Orlando John Hollis: The Verdict Is In

When Orlando Hollis announced that he was retiring after thirty-five years at the UO, twenty-five of them as dean of the law school, generations of lawyers turned over uneasily in their sleep. It was almost as though the Pope had resigned.

Dean Orlando John Hollis: the name alone evoked awe. A round, rolling, magisterial name, hinting of polished mahogany, hear ye's and therefores. It was all there even when he was a young professor, back in the '30s. Law students came under his amber stare and turned into gaping schoolboys, twisting their caps in their hands. If they escaped the eyes, they capitulated to the voice. Nobody could argue with the voice: nobody tried.

Let a student wander haplessly into some rhetorical quagmire, and Hollis was on them like a hawk. "There is a process we like to use in the practice of law, gentlemen. It is called *thinking*." And thinking was logical premise supported by fact. Pure, diamond-hard fact, uncolored with emotion, nailed so tightly into the form of argument that it became as unassailable as a concrete blockhouse.

His students called him a militarist, a Simon Legree, a hundred names unprintable. They sweat blood to meet his demands, cursed him over their midnight beer. And, they beat their heads against the wall of one inescapable truth: he was fair. "You had the feeling," said Justice O'Connell, "that if his own mother were involved in a judgment, it would make absolutely no difference to him. He had a purity of impartiality that is hard to equal."

It takes about ten years for most students to get over the sting of Hollis. The fear once inspired in students gets a new evaluation when entering professional life. "I've argued cases in front of the Circuit Court and in front of the Supreme Court," says Jack Faust, "and I've never felt as awed as I have been by Dean Hollis. You know that if you've done your briefing for a high court case as well as you would for the dean, you have nothing to fear."

Alumni speak of his cold professionalism during their student years. They freely admit their fear. But when he retired, they came by the hundreds from all over the state to honor him.

Why? Because he was an indelible part of their youth. Because in a world full of phonies, he came through as the genuine article. Because he was a great teacher. And, one suspects, because they loved him. Not that his former students would ever use such language. They have been too well schooled, by the dean himself, to permit any statement so sentimental.

—*Lucille Vaughn Payne*

"establishment" eating people and excreting soldiers, a blossoming grape boycott in the dorms, a confrontation with coaches over whether black athletes would be required to get haircuts, and the harassment of military and industrial recruiters—all brought out Johnson's critics in force.

"Stop the filth," Oregon Governor Tom McCall told Johnson. Letters from irate parents and taxpayers bombarded him daily.

The steps of Johnson Hall have been the site of various protests over the years, including this 1968 event.

"I was shocked and dismayed when I learned... My daughter came home and told me what's happening... I'm sick and tired of paying taxes to support... What I saw was sickening... You surely misread the public mind... The public is fed up to the eyeballs... Hippies, hoodlums, communists, nihilists, heathens... I intend to write every member of the Legislature... "

With these angry comments ringing in his ears, Charles Johnson died in a collision with a logging truck. Two months later Robert Clark, who had left the University to go to San Jose State, assumed the office of president.

As the '60s came to an end, there were 15,200 students on campus. Each day at the EMU, they bought 2,263 cups of coffee, cashed 345 checks (and bounced 10), ate 480 breakfasts, 1,700 lunches, and 1,400 dinners.

The division between established society and the new "youth culture" had grown. The atmosphere on campus was religious—pious and intoxicating, like a tent revival, with sharp pressure to convert or move on. A holy war was in the air. The sometimes violent energy that was focused on new approaches seemed inexhaustible.

Conversations at the EMU were intense, salted with references to Marcuse, Hesse, *The Greening of America*, Marx, relevance, the "student revolution."

"As I see it, the U.S. government today is not relating to the needs of the people. The power is in the people. That's you.

Therefore, you can use me for whatever you want. I'm your thing," ASUO Senate candidate Valerie Ingelo told student voters.

She was easy to pick out of a crowd—knee-high boots, miniskirt, brown hair, freckles, and two black eyes (souvenirs of confrontation with some of the more militant campus activists). She lost the election.

Several professors challenged the traditional grading system, either allowing students to grade themselves or simply giving everyone A's or B's.

"I don't buy the idea that there are absolute standards against which you can measure an individual," said Professor John Wish of the business school.

Classes on eastern religions were full, and there were waiting lists to get into anthropology courses. Professor Art Pearl of the education and sociology departments merged his "Alienation of Youth" course with another called "Can Man Survive?" The combined enrollment came to nearly 4,000 students with forty professors, who explored various aspects of human ecology. It was taught in McArthur Court because that was the only place large enough to hold it.

GOLDA WICKHAM: DEAR "MRS. W."

When Golda Wickham decided, in 1968, to retire after twenty-four years as dean of women at UO, the response from the campus community was just short of an uproar. Friends on campus gathered in praise of her humor and dedication to student welfare, alumni wrote letters, University officials extolled her virtues and contribution, campus and local press wrote glowing stories about Wickham's quarter-century of service to UO students.

Wickham, who before coming to UO had served as dean of girls at Portland's Lincoln High School and a teacher at Eugene High School (now South Eugene High School), was truly an Oregon native. Born in Leona, raised in Eugene and educated at the Oregon College of Education and the University of Oregon, she committed her career to the students of her native state.

During her time at UO, she was known for humor and goodwill. She set up an "Angel Fund" with donations from her own pocket, her friends and UO mothers to help students out in a pinch. Over the years, the fund gave out over $15,000 for trips home, glasses, shoes, books—even bail.

Her reputation wasn't limited to campus, however. Wickham was a star of Oregon's education system and community—there were even rumors that she should run for state legislature after her retirement. She was a president of the Portland Deans Association, Zonta and the Oregon State Deans, a member of the Oregon State Curriculum Committee, the AAUW State Scholarship Committee and countless other boards and committees.

But most important, both for Wickham and everyone who knew her, were her relationships with students. She kept track of them for years after graduation, and they wrote her letters, thanking "Dear Mrs. W." for her advice and support.

—*Jessica MacMurray*

Industrial and military recruiters continued to have a hard time. Navy recruiters were tried for "war crimes" in 1970 and demonstrators dropped plastic baggies of motor oil in a room occupied by Standard Oil representatives. More than fifty students disrupted a meeting held by representatives of the Weyerhaeuser Corporation. Western Kraft dropped the UO from its recruitment schedule.

In spite of the play the incidents got in the media, there were 56 percent more business administration degrees awarded that year than in previous years, and twenty University business students staged a counter-demonstration that spring. Their signs read: "Let them interview us."

President Clark was firm when faced with a 1968 sit-in.

To protest student arrests, police on campus, the ROTC vote and the war, approximately 100 students staged a sit-in in Johnson Hall.

On April 15, 1970, the faculty voted 199 to 185 to retain ROTC on campus. Angry, disappointed students marched on the ROTC classroom complex, doing considerable damage to French Hall. Several arrests followed. Hundreds of students marched on the Eugene City-County Jail to demand the release of those arrested. The demands were rejected.

To further protest the arrests, police on campus, the ROTC vote and the war, approximately 100 students staged a sit-in in Johnson Hall. President Clark called the police and sixty-three more were arrested.

The additional arrests angered members of the ASUO Senate, many of whom had been witnesses. They voted to support the student strike and boycott of classes that had been in effect since April 15, but ignored by many moderate students. The Senate action rallied another 1,000 students to the cause of the April 15th Committee.

On May 5, horrified by what had happened at Kent State the day before, an estimated 4,000 students and faculty joined in special activities. Almost as many marched down 13th Avenue that night as part of what *Old Oregon* staff writer Karen Place called "not just another peace march."

"In this time of mourning and sorrow, we must not turn away from the young as they stand before us and demand a new world where all men are brothers," said Robert Clark. "The blood of a new generation which has been spilled from Vietnam to Ohio is witness to the urgency of their pleas."

During April and May, the tension on campus had grown unbearable. Instructors sometimes broke down in front of their classes, and radical activists occasionally burst into the classrooms, exhorting, then berating uncommitted students who continued to attend classes during the strike.

Dozens of leafleteers were handing out flyers in front of the EMU, announcing the next rally, march or meeting. People with bullhorns were speaking almost nonstop from the Free Speech

Steve Prefontaine, UO's legendary track star.

Track Town, USA

Unlike many slogans attached to sports teams, Track Town USA is not marketing hype or wishful thinking. It is a reflection of a reality that took root in the Eugene community beginning in the 1950s and reaching full bloom in the 1960s.

When Bill Bowerman came to coach the UO track and field team in 1949, the program had a long history of regional success under long-time coach Bill Hayward. But Oregon had not made much of a mark on a national level, and track meets were long, dull affairs that didn't have much appeal for spectators. But Bowerman changed the pace of track meets, tightening the schedule of events so meets offered an exciting afternoon of athletic entertainment. He also made Eugene a city of participants. Shortly after becoming track coach, Bowerman started an all-comers meet for grade school athletes and later expanded it to include high school and college-age athletes. In 1957, he and North Eugene High School track coach Bob Newland formed the Emerald Empire Athletic Association (which later became the Oregon Track Club) to promote track, provide training and facilities and bring big meets to Eugene. By the early 1970s, 400 to 500 fans were used to seeing national championships and Olympic trials at Hayward Field.

While kids in other parts of the country pretended to be star football or baseball players, Eugene native and writer Mark Kirchmeier—who was nine years old when Oregon won its first national championship at Hayward Field in 1962—remembers that kids in Eugene would pretend to be mile runner Dyrol Burleson or other Oregon track stars. Runners—from Bill Dellinger to Burleson to Steve Prefontaine to kids at all-comers meets to men and women chugging slowly through our parks in the rain—became an integral part of Eugene's identity, something sure to make any thirty-second summary of what kind of city we are.

As track took hold in Eugene, the city was changing, too. A mill town with a small liberal arts college before the war, Eugene was slowly shifting to becoming more of a liberal arts college town with a timber-based economy. And "track is a liberal arts kind of sport," as Kirchmeier puts it. As postwar prosperity increased the mobility of Americans, more liberal arts types were attracted to Eugene's natural beauty and maverick spirit. And the nationally televised image of Pre—his hair flowing in the breeze his stride created—circling a roaring Hayward Field, and the camera occasionally straying to the majestic firs outside the field only added to Eugene's mystique. It's hard to measure how important that image was to the people who were attracted to Eugene in the great migration of the late 1960s and early 1970s, and how important those people are to the character of the city in the year 2000, but I believe that its influence was enormous.

UO track won four national championships under Bowerman, and the men's team won one under his successor, Bill Dellinger. The women's team, which wasn't even allowed to have meets at Hayward Field until 1972, won a national championship in 1985. Though most fans point to the 1970s as the end of the golden age of UO track, Eugene maintains an undeniable claim to the title of Track Town, and the UO athletes continue to perform at the highest levels of NCAA competition.

—*Guy Maynard*

platform, denouncing public officials, the war, corporations and various uncommitted or war-supporting institutions.

Eventually, many students stayed off campus altogether, committed neither to the right nor the left, but exhausted by the strain. By the time summer began, the ranks of the activists were also thinning. Some couldn't afford any more bail. Others were tired, frightened, frustrated.

In October 1970, a bomb exploded in Prince Lucien Campbell Hall at 9:20 P.M. It caused $50,000 of damage and PLC became one of nine bombed or damaged sites in Eugene. In December, a second bomb went off in the basement of Johnson Hall, causing another $9,000 damage. Early in February 1971, students learned that Robert Clark had turned over the names of 276 students to the FBI. The *Emerald* learned of it when Roy Rodgers, head of the sociology department, objected to the release. Rodgers, the *ODE* reported, had been approached earlier by the FBI, who claimed that someone in a sociology class titled "Critical Spirit" knew something about the bombings.

The exposure was embarrassing to Dr. Clark and hurt his credibility with the students.

That spring, a less extensive wave of protests and demonstrations resulted in a reported $2,500 damage (mostly in broken windows) by police estimates. As summer came, the activism dwindled and faded.

Eventually, the elimination of the draft destroyed most of the activists' base of support.

Many of the activists tried their hand at student politics, convinced they could change at least a part of the world. ASUO politics became noisy and hectic, with personalities discussed as much as the issues. Dirty politics alienated a great many of the rank-and-file students, now truly tired of *all* conflict.

President Clark retired in 1975 and was replaced by William Boyd, who had little apparent appetite for student activism.

"I don't view the University as an experiment in government," Boyd said, emphasizing that students weren't "in charge" anymore, if they ever were. Although many students will disagree, he said, the University is not a political operation.

"It's a scholarly enterprise," Boyd said, "and the student's principal role is as a learner."

While many students in 1976 agreed that it was a principal role, they were firm that it was not their only role.

Eventually, many students stayed off campus altogether, committed neither to the right nor the left, but exhausted by the strain. By the time summer began, the ranks of the activists were also thinning. Some couldn't afford any more bail. Others were tired, frightened, frustrated.

Robert D. Clark
President 1969–1975

In June 1969 the University, city and state were shocked by the death of Charles Johnson, the accounting professor and dean of liberal arts who had postponed a sabbatical to serve as acting president during the search for Arthur Flemming's successor. It had been a tremendously difficult year, one of demonstrations, protests and boycotts.

The eleventh president was to have little respite.

Robert Donald Clark had first come to the University in 1943, as an assistant professor of speech. He was a Nebraskan who had earned his B.A. at Pasadena College and his Ph.D. at the University of Southern California.

At Oregon he moved into administration: in 1956 he was appointed dean of the College of Liberal Arts and by 1962 he was dean of faculties. In 1964 he was offered the presidency of San Jose State College in California.

Both the race issue and protest against the Vietnam war surfaced during Clark's tenure at San Jose State. He developed a reputation for fairness and understanding; in 1966 he was one of the first college administrators to speak out against the war. When he announced his decision to accept the Oregon presidency, an assembly of San Jose students honored him with a long standing ovation.

A torchlight march was at the door of his home within weeks after his return to Eugene. He met with the students, he understood their concerns, was willing to talk to them, willing to reason with them—but he made it clear he would not let the University be destroyed by protests.

Clark understood student concerns, was willing to reason with them—but made it clear he would not let the University be destroyed by protests.

In the course of the school year 1969–1970, bombings, breakage, fires, and large-scale demonstrations reached the headlines. The state and the citizens reacted. Clark received hundreds of letters of advice on handling the protests, not all of it temperate. But because he refused to panic or overreact, he was able to face the governor, the legislature, the citizens and the intellectual community with an institution that had suffered but survived.

Since 1953 University enrollment had grown steadily; a sharp decline in 1972 forced the realization that the institution was facing a major financial dilemma. Federal funds, which the University had come to depend upon, were no longer readily available. Private gifts fell off. Inflation accelerated costs. And at this critical juncture, a 4 percent budget cut for state institutions of higher education was mandated by the Oregon legislature.

As a response to this crisis—which required an overall cut of nearly 10 percent in University expenditures—Clark created the Hearing Panel on University Priorities. Over many months the panel of administrators, faculty and students reviewed budget proposals from every segment of the University. Clark studied the final report and decided what programs must be cut. Not everyone was happy with the results, but the fairness of the process cannot be faulted.

The composition of HPUP was one instance of widening participation in University life and governance during Clark's six years on campus. Student involvement in the committee system was initiated. Women and minority students made gains, most tangibly in the creation of women's and ethnic studies programs. It was a good start, and long overdue.

When Clark retired in 1975—the first in a long line of Oregon presidents to retire in office—the Honors College that he had been instrumental in establishing in the 1950s and preserving in the tumultuous early 1970s was named in his honor. He was praised by many who had not agreed with his handling of the protests. Time, in this instance, had proven his actions correct.

Clark and his wife, Opal, continued to live in Eugene after his retirement from the University.

—*Jessica MacMurray*

UO's centennial, 1976.

Oregana *staffers of 1980 re-create the 1890 Senior Class Picnic (see page 9).*

Johnson Hall protest, 1986.

University Day, 1991.

Creating a New University

by Jamie Passaro

Tuition for the 1976-77 school year increased to $179 per term for undergraduate residents, up $18 from the previous year. The protests weren't anything like those of the early 1970s, but the students, many of whom had caught idealism from older siblings who had participated in Vietnam protests, were serious.

Students were taking more control over their education through student government. They had a well-spoken student body president in Jan Oliver, the first black ASUO president and second woman to hold the position. Oliver, at twenty-seven, was just a few years older than the average student—many of whom attended the University on the GI Bill.

Oliver became involved in student government because she was frustrated by the elimination of federal funding for the UO's childcare program and because newly appointed UO President William Boyd had, in one of his first acts as University president, closed the University's cultural centers. Boyd, a pleasant man with a soft Southern accent, was inaugurated in 1976 amidst applause, angry protests and police arrests. Oliver worked with Boyd to establish the Council for Minority Education, a more efficient restructuring of what had been the cultural centers.

Though campus traditions such as the homecoming dance, bonfires and the Canoe Fete had been cast aside—in part because they were seen as frivolous to an older, worldlier student body than the pre-Vietnam era one—students weren't serious and noble all the time. Elvis Presley appeared

---

"At the registration went to pay my fees Reached into my pockets, they said 'more money please':
Well I can't find a job, and that ain't too cool.
Now how the hell 'm I gonna stay in school"
— 1976 protest chant

The cast of Animal House, *filmed at the UO during the summer of 1976.*

on campus in two sell-out performances—both fundraisers for the athletic department. And the following ad appeared in the *Oregon Daily Emerald*:

> <u>Wanted for Feature Film</u>
> *Classic looking frat guys and sorority girls. Experience in film or theater absolutely essential.*

The UO signed a contract with Universal Studios to serve as the location for the filming of *National Lampoon's Animal House*. The studio turned the UO into Faber College, a 1962 party school, and hired hundreds of students and community members as extras. A white Victorian house on East 11th Avenue became the Faber chapter of Delta Tau Chi; the EMU Fishbowl was the site of the famous food fight scene; and President Boyd's office was used to film a scene in which the movie's protagonists delivered a horse to the Faber College president as a prank. Boyd's furniture was moved out for the scene.

Though the studio signed a contract that said it would not divulge the location of the film, the University still gets letters from around the world asking about it, and tourists still visit to see the setting for the famous John Belushi movie—although the house has been demolished.

The movie did touch on a trend, though. At the end of the 1970s Greek membership was on the rise again after disinterest in the 1960s. "Students have changed in contradictory ways," said President Boyd just before he left in 1980. "Students are more serious about their studies, almost to the point of grimness. But they're newly interested in the formality of the old fun and games of college life."

Despite intense budget cuts, academic life at UO thrived in the 1980s. Among 105 public universities in 1983, only five ranked higher in molecular biology, six in psychology and nine in biochemistry. In contrast, the UO was 101st in the level of state support per student. The percentage of state support dropped from 31 percent in 1980–81 to 29 percent in 1982–83.

William Beaty Boyd
President 1975–1980

As William Beaty Boyd took office in 1975, the University was entering a period of relative calm. After the tumult of the late 1960's and early 1970's, it seemed that the campus and the community were both ready for a gentle leader, a smoother ride and a stable administration. Boyd, and Provost Paul Olum who would succeed Boyd as president, provided all of these things.

Boyd arrived on campus just as the University was about to celebrate its centennial, and it was amid much celebration and hoopla that he was inaugurated in January of 1976. The University commissioned a composition from music professor Harold Owen, who wrote the *Centennial Variations & Finale* double wind quintet for Boyd's inauguration. During that year, the campus community and Eugene celebrated UO's hundredth birthday with the publication of the first *Atlas of Oregon*, a floating parade down the Millrace and a number of other events. While UO celebrated, the new president got to work.

Boyd reorganized the central administration by shifting some of the duties formerly handled by the president's office to the provost's office. He recognized the need for a new provost, and appointed Paul Olum to the post. Together, they moved the majority of the day-to-day academic operations to the provost's office, leaving Boyd free to reexamine minority programs, address budget concerns and streamline administration.

Boyd took a new stance toward political activism as well. As vice chancellor at the University of California, Berkeley from 1966 to 1968, Boyd became a student of student activism, and was firm in his belief that dramatic protest did more harm than it did good. At UO, the late 1960's and 1970's had been intense with protests and heated debate over issues on campus and off. But the students and faculty of the late 1970's worked for change from within—a tendency that Boyd was definitely behind. He encouraged student involvement at many levels of administration, from ad hoc committees to the collective bargaining table.

A believer in the power of higher education, Boyd was also committed to discouraging Oregon's high school students from heeding what he called the "siren call" of vocational schools. "The student who by liberal education has been liberated from poverty and parochialism of mind and spirit, who possesses sharpened analytical and descriptive skills, who has learned to learn, how to work hard, how to set and meet high standards, such a student will finally prevail in any economy," Boyd said. "And what's more, such students will live richer and more contributive lives on the job and elsewhere."

For the most part, Boyd's tenure at UO was free of controversy. But just as he was about to finish his term, a scandal erupted that put a sour end to an otherwise calm period. Fake transcripts and transfer credits were discovered in the football program, and Boyd reacted with fury. Coaches were dismissed; those that remained faced salary freezes and pay cuts.

Through it all, Boyd maintained a charismatic image on campus. Known for his eloquence and soft Southern drawl, Boyd was both a campus figurehead and an intensely private person. At once charming and introspective, he has been described as "Lincolnesque," and was well-liked on campus. After only five years as president, Boyd left office. He capped off his final commencement speech with a Kurt Vonnegut quote that was a theme throughout his presidency: "Damn it, baby, you've got to be kind."

—Jessica MacMurray

> *"The student who by liberal education has been liberated from poverty and parochialism of mind and spirit, who possesses sharpened analytical and descriptive skills, who has learned to learn, how to work hard, how to set and meet high standards, such a student will finally prevail in any economy."*

Creating a New University

MAJOR FACILITIES AND ADDITIONS * 1975–2001	
Name	Year
University Inn	1975
Education addition	1980
Agate Hall	1984
Millrace I and II	1986
Chiles Center	1987
Museum of Natural History	1987
Deschutes Hall	1990
Streisinger Hall	1990
Willamette Hall	1990
Cascade Hall	1990
Millrace III	1990
Casanova Center	1991
Bowerman Building	1991
Lawrence Hall addition	1991
Library addition	1992
Rainier Building	1993
Spencer View	1996
Willamette Block	1996
Moshofsky Center	1998
Knight Law Center	1999
Student Recreation Center	1999
Zebrafish Stock Center	2000
Student Tennis Center	2000
Graduate Housing	2001
*10,000 square feet or more	

In June of 1983, *Old Oregon*, the University's alumni magazine, quoted President Paul Olum as saying the University had pushed the miracle as far as it could. There were no salary increases for faculty between 1983 and 1985.

Still, the University managed to hire top-notch faculty in targeted disciplines. Faculty applied for more federal grants and outside funding to offset the dwindling state support. With the help of two U.S. senators, the University received $33 million in the '80s from the U.S. Department of Energy to construct new science buildings.

In 1985, for the first time in UO history, there were more women studying on campus than men—of 16,375 students, 8,234 were women. By contrast, in 1950, women made up just one-third of the student population. From the 1980s on, women began to appear regularly in the top three editorial positions at the *Oregon Daily Emerald*. And half of the ASUO presidents during the 1980s were women.

It was time for another pendulum swing in student government. A Greek and law student coalition dominated student government from the mid-1970s after Jan Oliver until groups of student activists banded together to form Students for a Progressive Agenda (SPA) in 1982.

Mary Hotchkiss was the first SPA-endorsed ASUO president in 1983–84. The twenty-nine-year-old English major and mother was tired of watching fraternity boys vote on child-care issues. She ran for the position wearing long braids and a "Women's place is in the House and Senate" T-shirt.

In the spring of 1984, Michi Ando, a sixty-three-year-old Denver schoolteacher, donned a cap and gown and participated in the UO's graduation ceremony forty years after her actual graduation. The federal government had denied Ando permission to participate in her 1943 graduation ceremony because it had set a curfew for people of Japanese descent. Forty years later, Keith Richard, the University's archivist, stumbled across documents about Ando (then Yasui). He initiated her return with a phone call and then a letter. When Ando returned to campus and gave a speech at graduation, the students, seated at Hayward Field, rose to their feet and gave her a standing ovation. It was a fitting beginning for an era when UO became known for Asian language studies, exchange programs and a growing international student population.

In 1986, business was the most popular major with 16 percent of UO students enrolled in the School. The average student was nearly twenty-five years old. Undergraduates were taking longer to graduate and more than two-thirds of the students worked at least part time. Ten percent of the students on campus were from countries other than the United States.

Record numbers of students came to campus in the late 1980s—18,350 in the fall of 1988—even as the cost of a college education had more than doubled in the past decade. Greek life enjoyed a resurgence as the seriousness of the '60s and '70s faded into memory. Toga parties were back, and with them old traditions: pinning, formal dances and even, briefly, the Canoe Fete. But as Greek life grew, the UO—and universities around the country—began to face hazing problems. On top of that, the gap between campus activists and the traditionally conservative Greek students widened.

BILL LOY: GEOGRAPHY GREAT

Bill Loy had no idea what he was getting into when he decided to create the first *Atlas of Oregon*. It was the early 1970s, and Loy had been an assistant professor of geography at UO for only a few years. He'd never undertaken so monumentally complex a task as compiling and organizing file cabinets full of information from hundreds of sources to tell the story of Oregon's sprawling 96,000 square miles: not only the story of its wildly varying surface geography, but also of its history, economy, geology and biology. Loy and his team built graphs, pie charts, bar charts, tables and illustrations from scratch; researched and wrote narrative text; meticulously handcrafted hundreds and hundreds of maps. After three years of consuming labor, the *Atlas of Oregon* was published in October 1976—on Loy's birthday, no less—to commemorate the UO's centennial.

For many people, such an arduous project would have been something to chalk up to experience, to tell war stories about. But Loy, this time as an emeritus professor, started again as the UO prepared to celebrate its 125th anniversary. In October 2001, again on Loy's birthday, the second edition of the *Atlas of Oregon* was published. Both editions were instant bestsellers, both garnered Loy and his collaborator, mapmaking virtuoso Stuart Allan, critical acclaim and academic reknown. The second builds on the concept of the first, taking new leaps with digital cartography. "We're picking the fruit of a tree we planted twenty-five years ago," beams Loy, as well known for his optimism and cheerful nature as he is for his tireless work ethic. "It would have been a shame not to take advantage of all that we learned the first time around. We're capable of so much more."

While Loy's atlases are a concrete legacy to UO geography and the state of Oregon, his impact on students has been deeply felt. A consummate teacher and perpetually positive force in the geography department, Loy is as loved as his books. In November 2001, the William G. Loy Undergraduate Teaching Lab was dedicated in Condon Hall.

—*Ross West*

Paul Olum
President 1980–1989

A sign hung in Paul Olum's office while he was president of the University of Oregon, reading, "The hottest places in hell are reserved for those who in a period of moral crisis maintain their neutrality." "It's up there because I believe in it so deeply," Olum said, "and it helps explain some things."

It explains a lot about Olum's nine years at the helm of UO. An expressive man with dark eyes and an easy conversational style, Olum spoke, at the end of his term, not about crises but about the quality of the UO.

"Oregon is in excellent shape, probably the best in history," he said. "We have a superior faculty in all respects all over the University, and we've gotten lots of good young people. The faculty is terrific and that's really the quality of the University," he said. "I think people love the place."

And, to an unusual degree, they loved Paul Olum. His presidency was marked by an uncommon respect for Olum among the faculty, staff, students and community, and great strides in the growth and national stature of the University.

He had his critics: those who thought a university president shouldn't take strong public stands on everything from apartheid and nuclear disarmament to state labor negotiations and the funding of higher education; those impatient with Olum's constant public reminders about the abysmally low level of state support for its universities.

But even his critics understood that Olum embodied the spirit of the academy. As president, he didn't just manage the University. He led by example, setting a tone of high ideals and academic excellence that helped keep a fine faculty in Eugene and attracted students who felt they were coming to one of the best public universities in the nation. When his forced retirement was announced, professors, students and community members reacted with an outpouring of support and affection unequaled in UO history.

The foundations of Olum's success at Oregon were laid early. Educated at Harvard and Princeton, Olum worked on the Manhattan Project before embarking on a distinguished career teaching mathematics. Olum specialized in algebraic topology, measuring and considering the shape of things, asking, for instance, what a doughnut and a needle have in common and what makes them different from a pretzel. For a quarter of a century, Olum taught and studied these concepts at the blackboards of Cornell University.

He left Cornell for a deanship at the University of Texas, but found an administrative standoff going on in Austin. Olum sided with the faculty, and quickly began looking for a new job. He found one at Oregon as the provost and vice president for academic affairs. When Bill Boyd resigned the presidency in July 1979, Olum stepped in as acting president and was named president soon after.

His time at Oregon was marked by astonishing growth, including twenty new research institutes and academic programs, which helped double the University's income through grants and contracts. He also began the most significant construction program in University history, which included a $34.6 million science complex and a $27 million remodeling of the library. His years were also marked by his trademark outspokenness, and eventually he was "retired" by the State Board of Higher Education, which called him "antagonistic." A rallying cry of support from people both on campus and off couldn't change the Board's decision, but it certainly solidified Olum's legacy as a beloved president.

—*Adapted from an article by David Arnold*

> *He led by example, setting a tone of high ideals and academic excellence that helped keep a fine faculty in Eugene and attracted students who felt they were coming to one of the best public universities in the nation.*

After dominating the ASUO for four years, the SPA lost the ASUO presidency in 1987 to Kasey Brooks, a former UO rally squad captain, sorority vice president, and daughter of the University's head football coach.

Many students believed the SPA had taken too much time working on noncampus issues such as apartheid in South Africa and a project with the University of El Salvador. "A number of students on this campus felt alienated," Brooks, a twenty-three-year-old law student, told UO's alumni magazine—sounding very much like Hotchkiss five years earlier. "I felt the focus had gotten a little bit out of whack." She won a tight race, campaigning on issues such as student health insurance, childcare, and parking.

In the fall of 1990, the University faced the most intensive budget threat in state history: Measure 5. The measure, which proposed to limit property taxes, threatened millions of dollars of lost tax revenue to the University—a fact that didn't seem to be on the collective mind of the student body. President Myles Brand called open forums to talk with students about the measure, but they wanted to talk about the Grateful Dead.

The band wouldn't be allowed to perform in Autzen Stadium as it had the spring before, the administration announced two weeks before Election Day. Responding to public concern that the Dead's concerts legitimized illegal drug use, UO Vice President Dan Williams banned the group from returning the next summer. Autzen Stadium, a landmark venue for the legendary band, would draw its fame not from music, but from football.

The 1990's at the UO were characterized by four trends: a growing athletic success, ongoing state budget cuts, increased private fundraising, and the incorporation of new technology. Duck football and women's basketball were the big stories. After a rough time in the 1980's, the football team became regionally and nationally known in the 1990's. Starting with the Independence Bowl in 1989, the Ducks made ten bowl appearances in thirteen seasons, including a disappointing loss in the 1995 Rose Bowl against Penn State. The Ducks of the 2000's don't show any sign of slowing down—a glorious victory at the 2001 Fiesta Bowl was capped off by a #2 national ranking and quarterback Joey Harrington's spot on the finalist list for the Heisman trophy.

Running back Saladin McCullough.

Star player Bev Smith (No. 24 above) returned in 2001 to coach the women's basketball team.

Creating a New University

> ### RESEARCH FUNDING
>
> In the last decade, University departments and programs received a remarkable number of major grants and contracts. These grants have allowed groundbreaking research in varying fields—and added immeasurably to the work done by professors and students on campus.
>
> | Year | Grant $(Millions) |
> |------|-------------------|
> | 1989–90 | $35M |
> | 1990–91 | $38M |
> | 1991–92 | $41M |
> | 1992–93 | $46M |
> | 1993–94 | $43M |
> | 1994–95 | $49M |
> | 1995–96 | $46M |
> | 1996–97 | $55M |
> | 1997–98 | $45.5M |
> | 1998–99 | $59M |
> | 1999–00 | $62M |
> | 2000–01 | $58M |
> | 2001–02 | $75M |

With the Ducks' success came fans. A long string of home-game sellouts led to a massive expansion of Autzen stadium, bringing capacity from 41,700 to 53,800 seats, begun the day after the 2001 season finished. Duck football also brought a new look to the UO—the sleek O that debuted on Duck helmets at the 1998 Aloha Bowl was so popular that the UO adopted it as an all-University logo in 2002.

At the same time, women's basketball began to enjoy success on the court and more fans than ever in the stands. Women's sports had slowly gained acceptance since the passage of Title IX in 1978. That year, Bev Smith, who is still considered one of the University's greatest athletes, began her basketball career at the UO. During her six years as a college athlete, Smith was named All-American twice. After years of coaching in her native Canada, Smith eventually returned to UO basketball, taking the helm of the women's team from Jody Runge in 2001. Runge had resigned after eight years as coach, a time marked both by serious controversy—Runge fought and won a much-publicized battle for salary parity, then her players campaigned for her resignation—and remarkable success on the court.

The 1990's brought more budget cuts balanced by private fundraising, athletic success and continuing academic prestige. Dave Frohnmayer was appointed president in 1994, and began a tenure characterized by a new level of accessibility. The age of technology brought change as well. Arena Registration, a grueling two-day registration ritual, ended in the fall of 1991. Since 1969, students had registered for classes by standing in long lines at Mac Court, followed by more lines in the EMU ballroom to pay fees. In the fall of 1991, when the last student walked out of Mac Court, Ralph Barnhard,

The long lines of arena registration were replaced with phone registration in winter 1992.

a senior chemistry instructor who had been in charge of registration for the chemistry department, uncorked several bottles of champagne. Duck Call, or phone registration, was introduced in the winter of 1992. Online registration was introduced in the winter of 2000. Though few will admit to missing Arena

Myles Brand
President 1989–1994

When the announcement came, in April 1994, that Myles Brand would become the next president of Indiana University, the reaction in Eugene was calm acknowledgement sprinkled with expressions of pride. His selection was not only a recognition of Brand's administrative ability but a compliment to the UO. Brand led the University through tough times, and his work did not go unnoticed.

After five years at UO, Brand left the institution in a position of strength to face the challenges of the 1990s. Chief among the challenges was finance: Brand oversaw a period of retrenchment and restructuring following 1990's Measure 5, putting in place a new tuition-driven budget that lessened the University's reliance on state funds. Although the UO continued to admit all qualified Oregonians, Brand encouraged aggressive recruitment of non-resident students. "He recognized that we had to become more entrepreneurial," said outgoing provost Norm Wessells.

Brand did not intend to rest his reputation on crisp spreadsheets when he arrived on campus in 1989. Administrators had expected public funding to remain relatively stable. Foremost on Brand's mind at the time was the graying faculty—about a third of whom could be expected to retire in the 1990s. Recruiting new faculty members would require paying nationally competitive salaries. When Measure 5 passed, Brand's vision of faculty recruitment had to change. Instead of hiring new faculty, he was faced with job cuts, program cuts and decreased enrollment numbers. Not everyone agreed with his decisions, but the changes had to be drastic to accommodate the budget cuts. In the end, 200 faculty jobs were lost and 22 academic programs cut.

Brand didn't allow the budget crisis to deter him from another of his priorities, however. He instated a campuswide planning process that resulted in a five-year strategic plan highlighting the importance of undergraduate education, an international curriculum, graduate student support, campus infrastructure and externally funded research.

Brand and the faculty also overhauled the structure of courses. The familiar three-credit class began its disappearance, replaced by the four-credit course that provides for greater in-depth study.

Following on the heels of the business and strategic plans was an academic productivity plan, completed in the spring of 1994. Brand and a 100-member faculty squadron led by math professor Charles Wright sought creative ways to increase enrollment without adding faculty. The plan aimed to give students more responsibility and encourage speedy graduation.

Brand's final act was a groundbreaker. The Oregon Campaign—which began July 1, 1992 and ended December 31, 1998—was the most ambitious and successful private fundraising campaign in the history of the University and the state of Oregon. During the campaign, private donors contributed a total of $255.3 million to the University of Oregon. The campaign surpassed its original goal of $150 million in 1996, established a new goal of $200 million, and exceeded that in December 1997.

Although the calm Myles Brand contrasted with his outspoken predecessor, Paul Olum, "his style very much fit the times," observed former dean of the College of Arts and Sciences Risa Palm. Brand piloted the University through rough waters and left in his wake what he called "a set of directions and focus" to guide the UO's next generation of leaders.

Brand left UO in 1994 to serve as the President of Indiana University—the equivalent to Oregon's Chancellor of Higher Education.

—*Mike Lee*

Brand piloted the University through rough waters, and left in his wake what he called "a set of directions and focus" to guide the UO's next generation of leaders.

Registration, it was a rite of the beginning of each term.

Beyond registration, technological advances in the 1990s changed the way students communicated with each other and with professors. Computer labs sprang up in every building on campus, as students and faculty alike recognized the benefits of being online. Dorms were wired so every student could be connected to the campus network from their room. Experimental online courses met with some success and by 2000, most courses included a website in their curricula where homework assignments and readings could be found, tests could be taken and class schedules could be posted.

Laptops, popular throughout campus, were required for law students starting in 1995.

GEORGE STREISINGER: FISH FOUNDER

George Streisinger is considered by many of his peers to be the founding father of zebrafish research. In the early 1970s, Streisinger determined that the zebrafish was a wonderful model for studying vertebrate development and genetics—a conclusion that had an enormous effect on genetic research worldwide.

Streisinger came to the University of Oregon by a circuitous route. In 1960, Streisinger had accepted a teaching position at Brandeis University. At a meeting that summer, he met Dr. Frank Stahl, a member of the University of Oregon's Institute of Molecular Biology, who convinced him to settle in Oregon instead. Streisinger soon formed a strong bond with the UO and with Oregon.

Streisinger's early research made major contributions in deciphering the genetic code, understanding the nature of frameshift mutations and the structure of the T4 phage genome. He dreamed of using the power of the same molecular principles to study the genetics and development of a vertebrate. He knew how easy it was to raise and maintain zebrafish: the fish was small enough to keep the large numbers required for genetic studies, but large enough to do classical embryological manipulations such as transplantations.

It was a daring change of course, and he was keenly aware of the critical views of his colleagues. It took almost ten years before he was ready to publish his first zebrafish paper.

Following Streisinger's death in a 1984 scuba-diving accident off the Oregon Coast, his lab members strove to further his mission. In a letter written one week later, one of his postdocs, David Jonah Grunwald, described the loss to the lab. "His range of interests, his willingness to reflect on the activities of others, and his generous spirit combined to make him a central force in guiding and maintaining the communal atmosphere of the Institute. "

His colleagues at the University of Oregon are still carrying on Streisinger's research. The proven research use of the zebrafish has spread to more than 300 developmental and genetics labs in more than thirty countries. Many of the mutant strains produced in the Streisinger Lab are still alive and being used towards providing answers to human and animal health issues—a well-deserved legacy for a true pioneer.

Streisinger Hall, part of the four-building Science Complex, is a permanent tribute to his work.

—*Pat Edwards, Charline Walker and Reda Kimmel*

1976–2001

HALLS OF SCIENCE

The $45.6 million science complex was dedicated in October of 1989. The four-building complex, funded through federal dollars, lottery funds and private donations, is a physical representation of the University's emphasis on interdisciplinary studies. Individual buildings are devoted to the traditional disciplines of physics, geology, computer science and biology. To promote and accommodate studies that break across traditional department lines, institutes such as molecular biology, chemical physics and neuroscience are located on a single floor and linked by bridges and walkways.

The science complex enhanced the University's already growing reputation as a center for interdisciplinary research and education. In 1991, the UO ranked tenth among the top twenty-five U.S. universities in both biological and physical sciences as measured by citations in research papers.

The atrium of Willamette Hall, above, and a view of the science complex from Franklin Boulevard, right.

Creating a New University

MUSEUM OF NATURAL HISTORY: KEEPER OF THE PAST

The University of Oregon Museum of Natural History unfolds mysteries about the natural sciences and human cultures past and present—from backyard birds and native trees to obsidian tools and cedar baskets.

The museum is the display, research and teaching facility for the Oregon State Museum of Anthropology collections, the University's Shelton and Prill zoological collections and the historic Condon Geology Collection. Also on hand are fossils, a saber-tooth tiger skeleton, and the world's oldest pair of shoes—a pair of sagebrush sandals discovered in 1938 by UO Professor Luther Cressman.

The building, funded by the University's late-1980's capital construction program, was dedicated in December 1987. Its construction reflects Pacific Northwest heritage, complete with thick rough wood beams and a copper salmon over the entrance.

Exhibits explore the archaeology and fossil history of Oregon, animals, plants and traditional human cultures. The museum also sponsors a variety of educational programs, events, and tours.

The late 1990s and early 21st century marked the passing of several UO—not to mention state and national—legends.

Bill Bowerman, the track coach who put Eugene on the map as Track Town USA, died on Christmas Eve of 1999 at age eighty-eight. Aaron Novick, founder of the UO Institute of Molecular Biology, died in December 2000 at age eighty-one. Novick was a renowned scientist whose work on the Manhattan Project during World War II disturbed him so much he spent the rest of his life campaigning against nuclear arms. Novick was dean of the UO Graduate School from 1971 to 1980 and head of the Department of Biology until his retirement in 1984. Paul Olum, UO's thirteenth and one of its most popular presidents, died in January 2000. He was eighty-two.

Eugene mourned again when Ken Kesey died in November 2001 at age sixty-six. Kesey, who wrote *One Flew Over the Cuckoo's Nest* and *Sometimes a Great Notion*, was described in an extensive *New York Times* obituary as "the Pied Piper of the psychedelic era." A 1957 UO graduate, Kesey returned to UO to teach a graduate writing seminar in which he collaborated with students on a mystery novel. "Caverns," was published under the pen name O.U. Levon (novel U.O., backwards).

Through the 1990s and into the 21st century UO student activists have continued to rally around causes, both on campus and off. The UO appeared on *Mother Jones* magazine's top ten list of student activist campuses three times between 1994 and 2001.

In April of 2000 students and community activists occupied the steps and lawn in front of Johnson Hall, demanding that the University join the Worker Rights Consortium, a new group set up to monitor conditions in overseas factories that produce University apparel. During the weeklong demonstration, fourteen people were arrested.

Jan Oliver, the 1976–77 ASUO president who is now a UO Associate Vice President, watched the demonstrations from her Johnson Hall office. Oliver looks back on the years of student government and sees former members of ASUO administrations in important positions in state and local government. "They go on to live lives that work so hard to be useful," she said. "I think it's one of the best things we do."

UO student volunteers registered more than 5,000 voters for the November 2000 election and brought Jesse Jackson, Gloria Steinem, Bill Bradley and the rock group Everclear to campus in get-out-the-vote efforts.

Dave Frohnmayer
President 1994–

"Knowledge is only gained through the continuing hard work and dedication that we have shown for the past century and a quarter. We aspire to transform lives through knowledge, each of us, every day."

When Dave Frohnmayer began his presidency in July 1994, the Eugene *Register-Guard* noted that the result was a "virtual love-fest on campus."

Why the celebration? For one thing, Frohnmayer was well known, both on campus (where he had been a law school professor, legal advisor to the UO president, and from 1992–94 a successful and admired Dean of the law school) and around the state (where he had served three terms in the Oregon House of Representatives and three more as Attorney General, earning recognition for his honesty and a record as the top vote-getter in state history). Medford-born Frohnmayer was also the first Oregon native to become UO president.

But he was more than a favorite son. Frohnmayer combined an impressive academic resume—undergraduate at Harvard, law at Berkeley and a Rhodes Scholarship at Oxford—with a reputation for accessibility, a commitment to building community and an ability to communicate the University's message to varied audiences. Dave (as he prefers to be known) could be both down-to-earth and highly professional, both humorous and inspiring. No wonder "Everybody loves Dave" became a catch-phrase at campus gatherings.

Frohnmayer's dedication to higher education led quickly to a number of new initiatives that would reshape the campus. His strong belief in undergraduate education helped to spur the UO's "Process for Change," a campus-wide planning effort that emphasized developing new approaches to more effective teaching. Diversity programs flourished and grew in number. His statewide reputation helped raise much-needed private funds. During his tenure the UO broke all existing Oregon fundraising records, garnering gifts for dozens of endowed teaching positions, scores of student scholarships, and a number of new academic programs (including Judaic Studies, the Warsaw Sports Marketing Center, Environmental Studies, and a new focus on entrepreneurship in the business curriculum). Frohnmayer has also been a bricks-and-mortar builder, bringing the campus a new law center, a new student recreation center, a zebrafish research center and major additions to the Museum of Art, College of Business Administration and Autzen Stadium, among other projects.

He also represents the UO nationally, serving on the NCAA board of directors and executive committee, as chair of the American Council on Education's Commission on Government Relations, and founding member of the Association of Pacific Rim Universities.

Two comments highlight Frohnmayer's attitude toward the UO. In his investiture speech, Frohnmayer spoke to the strengths of the University, and the tendency for the new president to try and reinvent the wheel. "We do not need a different University," he said. "But we must constantly dedicate ourselves to the development of a better one."

Then, in 2001, as the University celebrated its 125th anniversary, Frohnmayer focused the basic purpose of a university into a rallying cry for his faculty and staff. "Knowledge is only gained through the continuing hard work and dedication that we have shown for the past century and a quarter," he said. "We aspire to transform lives through knowledge, each of us, every day."

—*Tom Hager*

Creating a New University

When a record-breaking 19,000 students reached campus in the fall of 2001, the country was still bewildered over the September 11 terrorist attacks. The Concerned Faculty for Peace and Justice held a teach-in that drew thousands of students and community members.

In 2001–02, the UO celebrated its 125th anniversary by remembering those who, like Kesey, Olum, Novick and Bowerman, fought for the school and shaped its identity. Student life today is different in many ways, the same in others. On campus in 2001, students tap away on laptops at coffee shops, zip around on skateboards and chat on cell phones in Japanese and Arabic and Spanish. Instead of canoeing the Millrace, today's UO students take kayaks to the McKenzie and mountain bikes to the trails around Spencer Butte. The lively debate between traditionalists and political activists continues. The University still struggles to balance dwindling state funds with increasing enrollment and the growing cost of academic excellence. Students still challenge each other and the University, bringing new energy and perspectives with each incoming class.

JOAN ACKER: FEMINIST, SCHOLAR, ADVOCATE

For Joan Acker, study for study's sake is not enough. Acker, who has researched women, work and gender inequality for most of her forty years in sociology, strives to do research that will be of practical use to the communities that she studies. Her impact inspires for her students and colleagues and has changed the lives of women at work in Oregon and elsewhere.

In the 1980s she was on the State of Oregon Task Force on Pay Equity, helping with an exhaustive study of wage inequality among employees of the state. As a result of her work, many low-wage women workers saw pay raises. In 1999, Acker published a major work with the UO's Sandra Morgen. *Welfare Restructuring, Work & Poverty* looks at the results of welfare reform for a random sample of over 800 people who received financial assistance from the State of Oregon in 1998.

On campus, Acker's most significant contribution has been to help build the Center for the Study of Women and Society, an organization committed to promoting scholarship and disseminating worthy research to the academic community, the public and policymakers. As founding director, Acker set the tone for the center's work over almost three decades.

"She set a strong course from which the center has never veered," says Morgen, now the director of CSWS. "Her support of CSWS is unwavering and valuable."

Joan Acker has left a wake of serious scholarship, practical resources and committed activity both in the University community and the world of sociology. Acker has lived and studied all over the world, from Indiana to New York, Australia to Norway—but has kept Eugene and UO as her base through her remarkable career. She has received the Career of Distinguished Scholarship Award and the Jessie Bernard Award for feminist research from the American Sociological Association, as well as other fellowships and awards. Now partially retired, Acker remains actively involved in the sociology department and CSWS.

—*Jessica MacMurray*

1976 – 2001

GRADUATION STATISTICS
1876-2000

Bachelor's degrees conferred: 123,812

Master's degrees conferred: 40,743

Doctoral and Law degrees
conferred: 13,180

TOTAL: 177,735

MILESTONES 1976–2001

1976
UO celebrates its centennial.

BUS: James Reinmuth appointed dean.

J: Galen Rarick appointed dean.

LAW: Professor Hans Linde is appointed to the Oregon Supreme Court.

1977
J: The School's first computer lab is installed.

1980
Paul Olum named thirteenth president of the UO.

AAA: Philip Dole (architecture) and Marian Donnelly (art history) establish the Historic Preservation Program, the first degree program in historic preservation west of the Mississippi.

1981
AAA: Wilmot Gilland becomes dean.

J: Everette Dennis appointed dean.

LAW: Derrick Bell is appointed dean.

1982
CAS: Biology professor George Streisinger becomes the first scientist to clone a vertebrate.

AAA: School of Architecture & Allied Arts
BUS: College of Business
CAS: College of Arts & Sciences
ED: College of Education
J: School of Journalism & Communication
LAW: School of Law
MUS: School of Music

AAA: Department of Planning, Public Policy and Management (PPPM) formed by an amalgamation of Department of Urban and Regional Planning and Wallace School of Community Service and Public Affairs.

1984
Donald Duck named an honorary alumnus, and is presented a cap and gown in front of thousands of adoring fans.

1985
J: Professor Arnold Ismach appointed dean.

1986
BUS: Oregon Executive M.B.A. program begins offering classes in Portland.

LAW: Maurice Holland appointed dean.

1987
AAA: Oregon State Legislature approves $8.03 million for the long awaited additions and alterations building construction project.

1989
President Olum resigns. Myles Brand named fourteenth president of the UO.

1991
CAS: Risa Palm appointed dean. New four-building science complex opens.

MUS: Department of Dance merges administratively with the School of Music.

ED: Measure 5 forces major program cutbacks, including the major in Curriculum & Instruction and elementary and secondary teacher licensure programs. College of Education faculty cut by 39 percent.

1992
Athletics Hall of Fame founded.

ED: Martin J. Kaufman appointed dean. COE begins extensive reorganization. After initial reductions from five divisions to two, departments are established and new undergraduate educational studies and licensure programs launched.

LAW: Dave Frohnmayer is named dean.

1993
J: School of Journalism is renamed The School of Journalism and Communication.

LAW: Registrar Lois Ackerman retires after fifty years at the Law School.

1994
President Brand resigns. Dave Frohnmayer named fifteenth president of Oregon. University launches the Oregon Campaign, the state's largest fundraising drive ever.

BUS: College of Business Administration renamed Charles E. Lundquist College of Business.

J: Duncan McDonald replaces Arnold Ismach as dean. The School adds a doctoral program in Communication and Society. The first annual Minority Workshop for high school students is held.

LAW: Law and Entrepreneurship program is established. Dean Dave Frohnmayer resigns to assume University presidency. Chuck O'Kelly is appointed interim dean.

1995
LAW: Twenty-five million dollar building campaign begins. The Appropriate Dispute Resolution Center is established.

1996
The Oregon Campaign surpasses $150 million goal two years early, sets new goal of $200 million.

CAS: Joe Stone is appointed dean.

1997
LAW: Rennard Strickland is appointed dean.

1998
The Oregon Campaign ends after raising $255.3 million.

J: Professor Tim Gleason replaces Duncan McDonald as dean after McDonald becomes University vice president for public affairs and development.

1999
BUS: Philip J. Romero appointed dean.

ED: First group of COE graduates since Measure 5 receive full licensure and master's degrees in Education. Middle/Secondary teacher training program established.

2000
UO ranked No. 1 public university for having the most students enrolled in international and travel abroad programs. Graduating class reaches 4,265 students.

THE OREGON CAMPAIGN

In 1988, President Olum kicked off a fundraising campaign called The Campaign for Oregon by announcing a gift from Phil Knight, UO alumnus '59 and co-founder of NIKE, toward a $24.7-million renovation of the UO main library. In 1996, Knight gave $25 million to the program's sequel, the Oregon Campaign. It was the largest gift in UO history, allocating $15 million for new endowed chairs and professorships and $10 million for a new law school building.

The Oregon Campaign, pet project of University Vice President Brodie Remington, sought to answer the crises inflicted by Measure 5. Remington and President Myles Brand were convinced that the UO had to shift from being a "state-supported university" to a "state-assisted university"—looking to private donations and fundraising campaigns for funding, instead of state money.

The Oregon Campaign began in 1992 with a six-year strategy and a goal of $150 million. In 1996, the Campaign surpassed that goal, and set a new one at $200 million. The University's most ambitious and successful fundraising campaign ever ended in 1998 with a total of $255.3 million raised in pledges and gifts. Thirty-one million dollars went for student scholarships, fellowships, and other financial aid. Approximately $63 million was raised to support the faculty; much of it went to endowed chairs, which increased from twenty in 1991 to seventy-five in 1998. The Oregon Campaign raised $47.7 for building projects, including the William W. Knight Law Center, the Ed Moshofsky Sports Center, the Vivian Olum Child Development Center and renovation projects in Allen and McKenzie Halls.
—*Jessica MacMurray*

2001
University of Oregon celebrates 125th anniversary. For third consecutive year, the UO is listed in the Fiske Guide to Colleges as one of the nation's "best buys." UO freshman class grade point averages—3.43–are higher than any freshman class ever.

MUS: Bach Festival CD wins Grammy Award.

Notable Ducks

From *Making a Difference: 125 Years and Counting* by Jim McChesney

OREGON'S NO. 1 ALUMNUS?

He made the cover of *Time* magazine; he became president of a major rail company and a top diplomat for his nation. He was named UO's No. 1 Alumnus in 1933—but was accused of being a war criminal in 1946. After Yosuke Matsuoka, LL.B. 1900, graduated from the UO law school in Portland, he returned to Japan. There he defended Japan's seizure of Manchuria in 1931, supported his nation's Far East policies, promoted Japan's alliance with Germany and negotiated a nonaggression pact with Stalin. Following the war, Matsuoka faced war crime charges but died before the court reached a verdict.

REDS

When she attended the UO, Louise Bryant '08 was active in the women's suffrage movement, but it was not until she went to Russia in 1917 with her husband John Reed that she became caught up in revolutionary events that would shape the world for the rest of the century. She related her adventures in *Six Red Months in Russia* and was played by Diane Keaton in the movie *Reds*.

THE FRONT PAGE

In 1915 Lucille McDonald '23 aspired to be a reporter. At the *Eugene Guard*, she was told to "go get a story"; then they would decide whether or not to hire her. She came back with a baseball preview that wowed the editors and was hired on the spot, thus beginning an illustrious journalism career. McDonald was the first female copy editor in the Northwest, the first woman on a New York copy desk and the first woman night editor for United Press International in South America.

SHALL WE DANCE?

May Josephine Shelly '26 and Martha Hill, who taught at the UO from 1927 to 1929, co-founded the famous Bennington College Summer School in the 1930s. One of the first to promote the new forms of modern dance, the school employed instructors Martha Graham, Ruth Bloomer and Gertrude Shurr. Bloomer and Shurr taught at the UO in the 1930s and 1940s before reshaping Bennington into its current format, the American Dance Festival.

Alumni Facts

UO grads in major public service positions:
- 8 Oregon governors
- 7 U.S. senators
- 11 U.S. representatives
- 2 members of presidential cabinets

More than 140 Fulbrights
2 Nobels
9 Pulitzers
67 Olympic track & field athletes, since 1908
44 who have attained the rank of general or admiral in the U.S. Armed forces

Faculty Awards

1,846 Faculty members at UO in 2000-2001
180 Fulbright Scholars
53 Guggenheim Fellows
1 MacArthur Foundation genius grant recipients
6 American Academy of Arts and Sciences members
6 National Academy of Sciences members
1 Howard Hughes medical investigator
2 American Cancer Society research professors

TERMS OF ENDEARMENT

It's hard to separate Maurine Neuberger '29 from Richard Neuberger '35, because the one moved so perfectly to fill the gap left by the other. Both attended the UO, both served in the Oregon legislature, both were Democrats, and both were elected to the U.S. Senate. But when Richard died in 1960 with a year remaining in his term, Maurine was not named to complete it. She ran on her own the next year and won, becoming the first female to be elected to the Senate without first having replaced her husband.

WASHINGTON MONUMENT

Chloethiel Woodard Smith '32 made her mark on the nation's capital. Known for large-scale residential projects and office buildings, her design of the office building at Washington Square is thought by some to be the best in the city. In D.C., she pioneered the incorporation of new and historic buildings in the same project.

MAVERICK

When Tom McCall '36 won the Oregon governorship in 1967, he was the right person in the right place at the right time. Whether protecting beaches for future generations, eliminating massive pollution of the Willamette River or straight-talking out-of-staters with his admonition to "visit but don't stay," McCall was a political maverick who placed public good above party loyalty. He is one of eight UO alumni who have been elected state governor.

IN DER FUHRER'S FACE

For Mack Robinson '41, coming in second still made him a champion. A star UO sprinter in the late 1930s, Robinson competed in the 1936 Munich Olympics and, with Adolf Hitler watching, defeated the "supermen" in the 100-yard dash. Though Robinson finished second to Jesse Owens, together they showed the world the lie behind Hitler's ideas of racial superiority. Robinson was rated the best runner in the world in 1938—something his younger brother, baseball great Jackie Robinson, was proud of.

THE SHAPE OF THINGS

Thomas Hardy '42, M.F.A. '52, is an internationally acclaimed sculptor, who has works shown at the Metropolitan Museum of Art and the Whitney Museum. His work includes *Steelheads*, in downtown

Eugene's park blocks, and *Birds in Flight*, at Lloyd Center in Portland. He created artwork for the presidential seal at the Franklin D. Roosevelt Memorial in Washington, D.C.

MVP

In the late 1940s, Norm Van Brocklin '49 M.S. '51 *was* football at UO. Drafted by the pros after leading the Ducks to a 1948 Cotton Bowl, he led the L.A. Rams and the Philadelphia Eagles to league championships. With the Eagles over the Green Bay Packers, Van Brocklin became the only quarterback to defeat a Vince Lombardi team in a title game. He was named the NFL MVP in 1960.

AROUND THE WORLD

Among the UO grads who have risen to the top of diplomatic careers are Glen Holden '51, ambassador to Jamaica; Carol Hallett '59, ambassador to the Bahamas; Victor Tomseth '63, ambassador to Laos; and Kent Wiedemann, M.A. '73, ambassador to Cambodia.

A ROOM WITH A REVIEW

When the understated elegance and precisely fashioned lives of the characters in *Howards End* or *A Room with a View* come to the screen, it is because James Ivory '51 did not become an architect. Instead, this director, whose films have received Academy Awards, earned a B.F.A. at the UO—a degree he used to acquire an exquisite understanding of the way a film should look.

MR. SPEAKER

In 1972, Emery Barnes '54 was elected to the British Columbia legislature. He was a founding member of the B.C. black historical and cultural society. In 1994 he took his fight for rights and respect to a new position, Speaker of the Legislative Assembly, thus becoming the first African American to be elected speaker.

JEREMIAH WAS AN ADMIRAL

Admiral David Jeremiah '55 became the nation's number-two military man in 1990 when he was named vice-chair of the Joint Chiefs of Staff. Prior to becoming one of the military's top brass, Jeremiah commanded destroyers, squadrons and the U.S. Pacific Fleet. In 1986 it was his command that oversaw the capture of the hijacked *Achille Lauro*. Jeremiah stands as an example of the forty-four UO grads who have reached the rank of admiral or general—making the UO one of the top producers in the country, per capita, of senior military officers.

CHIEF EXECUTIVE OFFICER

Ken Smith '59, a Wasco tribe member, was the second Native American to graduate from the UO. Since then, he has served as CEO of the Confederated Tribes of Warm Springs and, during the Reagan administration, as a leader in the Bureau of Indian Affairs.

IN THE CABINET

Among UO graduates who have held positions of leadership and public service, two have made it to the U.S. president's cabinet: Neil Goldschmidt '63, who served as secretary of transportation for Jimmy Carter; and Donald Hodel, J.D. '60, who was secretary of the interior for Ronald Reagan. Goldschmidt also served as mayor of Portland and governor of Oregon.

M.P. AND MORE

As a parliamentary and cabinet member in the Republic of China, Yung Wei, M.A. '63, Ph.D '67, used his academic knowledge to introduce administrative and constitutional reforms at home. He has been a professor of political science at the National Chiao-tung University, president of the Vanguard Institute for Policy Studies and president of the Sino-American Cultural and Economic Association of the Republic of China.

BROADCAST NEWS

Behind the flickering screen of the NBC peacock, behind Tom Brokaw, behind the live feed from Jerusalem or the extended coverage of a presidential trip, is producer Margie Lehrman '66. In more than three decades of work, Lehrman has moved from researcher and associate producer of the *Today* show to her current position as senior Washington producer for special coverage.

STRUCTURAL INTEGRITY

As principal designer of the Smithsonian Museum of the American Indian, Native American architect Johnpaul Jones '67 works to create an integration of design and the historical spirit appropriate to the structure. His projects—including the Columbia River Gorge National Scenic Area Recreation Overview, the Portland International Airport Parkway and the Africa Project at Portland's Washington Park Zoo—illustrate his ability to bring art and construction into forms that serve more than function.

AD MAN

The list of clients includes such business behemoths as Microsoft, Coca-Cola, Miller Beer, ESPN and NIKE, Inc. In addition to its Portland headquarters, Wieden + Kennedy boasts offices in London, New York, Tokyo and Paris. Behind it all is Dan Wieden '67, who has hoisted the small company onto the top rungs of international advertising.

DESKTOP GUTENBERG

What Johann Gutenberg did for publishing in the fifteenth century is analogous to what Paul Brainerd '70 did for publishing in the late twentieth century. As founder of Aldus and developer of PageMaker software, Brainerd revolutionized publishing and made desktop publishing a household phrase.

LANDSCAPE AND IMAGINATION

From *Wolves and Men* to *Crow and Weasel*, *Arctic Dreams* to *Light Action in the Caribbean*, the books of Barry Lopez '70 shift in geographic locale, story genre and content in ways that belie single authorship. Yet Lopez writes all of them with a moral sense that is inescapably his—a sense that creates a framework for his vision of hope in the midst of dilemma, the need for personal integrity in the face of life's puzzles and the willingness to accept responsibility in the midst of paradox.

BUT I KNOW WHAT I LIKE

Art has long been controversial. But few have stood in the middle of the "what is art?" controversy as squarely as John Frohnmayer, J.D. '72. He headed the National Endowment for the Arts from 1989 until his resignation in 1992, following the NEA's controversial funding of the exhibit Tongues of Flame. Defending the right to freedom of expression, Frohnmayer described his experience in his book, *Leaving Town Alive*.

FROM DUCK TO VIKING TO PEACOCK

Ahmad Rashad '72 carried the football for huge yardage at the UO. He did the same as a running back for the Minnesota Vikings and became one of the team's top running backs ever—second in all-time scoring for Minnesota with fifty touchdowns in an NFL career that spanned from 1972 to 1982. Today Rashad carries the ball for NBC Sports as a commentator.

ECONOMIC ADVISER

When Vicente Fox's National Action party broke the seventy-one-year reign of Mexico's Institutional Revolutionary Party in 2000, he promised to transform Mexico. To provide leadership in the economic arena, Fox named UO grad Luis Ernesto Derbez, M.A. '74, to the cabinet-level post of head of the Ministry of Economy. Derbez has spent nearly twenty-five years as an economic adviser to the World Bank; he now stands ready to make history in Mexico's new government.

CONDUCT BECOMING

Randy Shilts '75 carved a place in journalism that was not simply groundbreaking but internationally influential in changing the way the news media covered AIDS. As the first openly gay reporter for a major newspaper, the *San Francisco*

Chronicle, Shilts was the first reporter to cover the AIDS epidemic full-time. From his first book, *The Life and Times of Harvey Milk* to *And the Band Played On* and *Conduct Unbecoming*, Shilts wrote with courage and truth.

STONE SOUP

Nationally syndicated cartoonist Jan Eliot '77 sees her craft as one of bringing humor amid the struggles of daily life. Eliot's cartoon, *Stone Soup*, appears in 138 newspapers across the U.S.

PAR FOR THE COURSE

Native Oregonian and PGA Tour golfer Peter Jacobsen '77 is driven by values and commitment to the people and purposes in his personal and professional life. Through twenty-three years of professional golf, he has remained an advocate for the state of Oregon, the city of Portland and the UO.

YESTERDAY AND TODAY

It didn't start out as bright lights and big cities for Ann Curry '78, news anchor for NBC's *Today*. She traversed from Ashland, Oregon, through the journalism school to early jobs at television stations in Medford, Portland and Los Angeles. When NBC tapped her for the coveted news anchor position on the *Today* show she became one of the first exceptions to the forty-eight-year tradition of male anchors on the show.

SEEKING CHANGE

When Diana Akiyama '81 became the world's first Japanese American to be named an Episcopal priest, she brought sensitivity to racial, ethnic and women's issues as well as a deep interest in the spiritual dimensions of human problems.

ENDURANCE

For Ann Bancroft '81, the trail to the North and South Poles began in the UO's physical education department. After becoming the first woman to ski to both poles, Bancroft set her sights even higher. In 2001 she and fellow explorer Liv Arnesen became the first women to ski and windsail across Antarctica.

MARATHON MAN

Alberto Salazar '81 won the Boston Marathon and set a world record in 1981—two hours, eight minutes, thirteen seconds. Salazar's record came in the midst of three consecutive wins at the New York Marathon in 1980, 1981 and 1982.

WRENCHING STORIES

When Chuck Palahniuk '85 traded his $5-an-hour newspaper job for thirteen years of twisting wrenches on diesel engines, he didn't let the stories in his head get away. One of those stories became the novel *Fight Club*, which was optioned in 1995 for a Twentieth Century Fox film starring Brad Pitt, Edward Norton and Helena Bonham Carter. Palahniuk has followed with *Invisible Monsters*, *Survivor* and *Choke*.

MORE *Facts* & FIGURES

UO BY THE NUMBERS 2001

295 acres of campus
77 undergraduate majors
57 undergraduate minors
120 master's programs
49 Ph.D. and doctoral programs
23 certificate programs
15,196 undergraduates
3,895 graduate students
46.7% of undergraduates are male, 53.3% are female
46.2% of graduate students are male, 53.8% are female
69.4% are Oregon residents
30.6% are nonresidents
7.5 % are international students representing 79 countries
8.3% are in the School of Architecture & Allied Arts
56.1% are in the College of Arts & Sciences
10.7% are in the College of Business Administration
7.4% are in the College of Education
7.1% are in the School of Journalism and Communication
2.7% are in the School of Law
2.7% are in the School of Music
0.3% are in interdisciplinary studies
5.1% are unclassified
20.9: median age of undergraduates
28.3: median age of graduates
18.9: median age of freshmen
2.25 million volumes in University Library holdings
23 languages taught on campus

THE UNIVERSITY SEAL
Created by Judge Matthew Deady, the seal features a drawing of Mt. Hood and the University's motto: *Mens Agitat Molem* (Mind Moves Matter).

THE DUCK
Early Oregonians were dubbed "Webfoots" because of Oregon's wet winters. At UO, the term was used first for the yearbook title in 1902, then as a nickname for athletic teams beginning in 1932. When drawings of the Webfoot began to resemble a popular Disney character, Walt Disney gave his permission to use Donald Duck as the official UO mascot.

THE FIGHT SONG
Mighty Oregon was written by band director Albert Perfect with student Dewitt Gilbert. The song was first performed on March 4, 1916. Over the years, lyrics have been altered to reflect current sensitivities, hence the old and new versions below.

MIGHTY OREGON
(original 1916 lyrics)
She is small, our Alma Mater
But she rules with strength and right.
What she lacks in mass and numbers,
She makes up for in her fight.
Oregon is never beaten
'Till the final whistles call.
Who can tell her tale of triumph?
Scores can never show it all.

Oregon, our Alma Mater,
We will guard thee on and on.
Fellows gather round and cheer her,
Chant her glory Oregon.
Roar the praises of her warriors,
Sing the story Oregon
Down the gridiron urge the heroes,
Of our Mighty Oregon.

Randy fellows, stand behind them,
They are doing all they can.
Back the team in sun and shadow,
Back the captain, back each man.
They will carry home the vict'ry
To old Deady's hallowed hall.
Give the team the best that's in you,
Give your Alma Mater all.

MIGHTY OREGON
(circa 2000)
Oregon, our Alma Mater
We will guard thee on and on
Let us gather round and cheer her
Chant her glory Oregon
Roar the praises of her warriors,
Sing the story Oregon
On to victory urge the heroes
Of our Mighty Oregon!

INDEX

A
Acker, Joan 96
Agate Hall 86
Akiyama, Diana 104
Allen, Eric 49
Allen Hall 36
Aloha Bowl 90
Alpha Tau Omega 66, 72
American Bar Association 43
American Medical Association 12
Animal House 84
Architecture and Allied Arts, School of 42, 43, 60, 70, 71, 98
Architecture and Fine Arts 37
Arena Registration 90
Arts and Sciences, College of 42, 60, 98
ASUO 24, 42, 77, 78, 80, 83, 86, 89
Autzen Stadium 29, 72, 89, 90

B
Bancroft, Ann 104
Barnes, Emery 102
Beall, Robert Vinton 71
Bean Complex 72
Beta Epsilon 26
Bezdek, Hugo 33
Black Panthers 75
Board of Regents 4, 11, 14, 15, 27, 30
Bowerman, Bill 68, 79, 94
Bowerman Building 86
Boyd, William Beaty 71, 80, 83, 85
Boyer, Clarence Valentine 48, 51, 60
Brainerd, Paul 103
Brand, Myles 89, 91, 98, 99
Brattain, Walter 70
Briggs, Cap 29
Brocklin, Norm Van 102
Bryant, Louise 100
Business, College of 42, 43, 60, 70, 71, 98

C
Campbell Hall 36
Campbell, Prince Lucien 20, 25, 31, 38, 42, 61
Canoe Fete 20, 36, 50, 53, 87
Carlson, Spencer 65
Carson Hall 66
Carson, Luella Clay 16, 17
Casanova Center 86
Cascade Hall 86
Center for the Study of Women and Society 96
Chapman, Charles Hiram 11, 13, 14, 16, 17
Chiles Center 86
Civil War 50
Clark, Robert Donald 71, 76, 78, 80, 81
Collier House 11, 43
Columbia Hall 72
Columbus Day Storm 68
Community Service and Public Affairs 74
Computing Center 72
Condon Geology Collection 94
Condon Hall 36, 87
Condon Oaks 10
Condon, Thomas 21
Council for Minority Education 83
Cravens, J.C. 40
Curry, Ann 104

D
Daily Emerald 24
Deady Hall 14, 15, 19
Deady, Matthew 14, 105
Dellinger, Bill 79
Derbez, Luis Ernesto 103
Deschutes Hall 86
Disney, Walt 60, 71, 105
Donald Duck 98, 105, *see also:* Mascot
Douglass, Matthew 61
Duck Call 90
Duck Preview 64
Dunn, Frederick S. 19

E
Earl Complex 72
Edgington, Grace 38
Ed's Coed 40
Education Building 36
Education, College of 42, 98
Eliot, Jan 104
Emerald Hall 59
Erb, Donald M. 56, 60
Erb Memorial Student Union 54, 72, 76, 84

Esslinger Hall 71
Eutaxian Literary Society 8

F
Fenton Hall 28, 36, 43, 61, 63
Fiesta Bowl 89
Flag Rush 19, 20
Flemming, Arthur Sherwood 68, 70, 74, 81
Freshman Bonfire 22, 32, 36
Friendly Hall 15, 23, 27
Friendly, Samson H. 15
Frohnmayer, Dave 71, 90, 95, 98
Frohnmayer, John 103
Frosh cap 25
Frosh week 65
Fuller, R. Buckminster 70

G
Gerlinger Annex 72
Gerlinger Hall 30, 36
Gerlinger, Irene Hazard 30
Gilbert, Dewitt 105
Gilbert Hall 36
Gilbert, James H. 41
Goldschmidt, Neil 102
Good Samaritan Hospital 12
Graduate Housing 86
Graduate School 30, 67
Grateful Dead 89
Gregory, Laird H. 52
Guppy, M. Ruth 30

H
Hall, Arnold Bennett 38, 43, 47
Hall, Gus 69, 74
Hallett, Carol 102
Hamilton Complex 72
Hardy, Thomas 101
Harris, Leo 60
Hayward, Bill 26, 28, 33, 41, 79
Hayward Field 29, 36, 38, 42, 79
Henderson, J.H.D. 14
Hendricks Hall 36
Hill, Martha 100
Hobson, Howard 52
Hodel, Donald 102
Holden, Glen 102
Hollis, Orlando 54, 59, 60, 71, 75
Homecoming 34, 36, 40, 50, 64, 69
Honors College 70, 81
Howe baseball field 51

Huestis Hall 72, 73
Huestis, Ralph 73
Hunter, Frederick 59

I
Independence Bowl 89
Independent Students' Organization 53, 57
Inter-Fraternity Council 73
Ivory, James 102

J
Jacobsen, Peter 104
Jeremiah, Admiral David 102
Johnson, Charles 71, 74, 75, 81
Johnson Hall 33, 36, 40, 71, 75, 80, 82, 94
Johnson, John Wesley 4, 13, 14
Jones, Johnpaul 103
Journalism and Communication, School of 42, 49, 60, 70, 71, 98
Junior Exhibit 17
Junior Flag Rush 17, 20
Junior Weekend 20, 36, 50, 64

K
Kappa Kappa Gamma 66
Kappa Sigma 26
KDUK 66, 70
Kelly, Dan 28, 33
Kesey, Ken 94, 96
Kincaid Field 25, 26
Kincaid, Harrison 49
Klamath Hall 72
Knight Law Center 86
Knight Library *see:* Library
Knight, Phil 99
KWAX 66

L
Laurean Literary Society 8, 9
Law, School of 14, 42, 43, 60, 70, 71, 98
Lawrence, Ellis 37, 61
Lawrence Hall 36
Leader, Colonel John 34
Lehrman, Margie 102
Librarianship, School of 74
Library 37, 43, 51, 61, 70, 72, 86, 88
Lopez, Barry 103
Loy, Bill 87

M
Marching Band 42
Mascot 28, 60, 71, 98, 105, *see also:* Donald Duck
Matsuoka, Yosuke 100
McArthur, Clifton (Pat) 24, 39
McArthur Court 35, 36, 38, 39
McCall, Tom 76
McClure Hall 49
McDonald, Lucille 100
McMahon, Mildred 66
Measure 5 89, 91, 99
Medical School 12
Mens Agitat Molem 4, 105
Mighty Oregon 42, 60, 105
Millrace 15, 25, 26, 41, 53, 57, 63, 64
Millrace Complex 86
Miner Building 59
Morse, Wayne 55, 60
Moshofsky Center 86
Mother Jones 94
Murphy, William Parry 60
Museum of Art 37, 67
Museum of Natural History 86, 94
Music Building 36
Music, School of 14, 42, 43, 60, 70, 71, 98

N
NCAA Basketball Championship 52, 60
NCAA Track Championship 29, 70
Neuberger, Richard 101
Neuberger, Maurine 101
Newburn, Harry Kenneth 59, 60, 70
NIKE, Inc 68, 99
Nobel Prize 70, 101
Noise Parade 36, 50, 58
Novick, Aaron 94, 96

O
Old Oregon 86
Oliver, Jan 83, 94
Olum, Paul 85, 86, 88, 94, 98
Olympians 28
Onyx Bridge 72
Oregana 42, 71, 82
Oregon Agricultural College 36, *see also:* Oregon State University
Oregon Campaign 91, 98, 99
Oregon Daily Emerald 42, 86
Oregon Emerald 32, 42

Oregon Hall 72
Oregon Monthly 42
Oregon State University 47, 50, 54, 64, 67, *see also:* Oregon Agricultural College
Oregon State Museum of Anthropology 94
Oregon Track Club 79
Oregon Weekly 24, 32, 42

P
Palahniuk, Chuck 104
Peace Corps 69, 72, 74
Perfect, Albert 42, 105
Phi Beta Kappa 42
Phi Delta 36
Phi Kappa Psi 69
Phi Sigma Kappa 64
Pi Kappa Alpha 64
Pioneer Father 40
Pioneer Mother 58
Prefontaine, Steve 71, 79
Prince Lucien Campbell Hall 71, 72, 80
Proctor, Alexander 40, 58

R
Rainier Building 86
Rashad, Ahmad 103
Reflector 42
Regents *see:* Board of Regents
Remington, Brodie 99
Robinson, Mack 101
Rose Bowl 33, 38, 62, 89
ROTC 35, 42, 48, 56, 71, 78
Runge, Jody 90

S
Salazar, Alberto 104
Science complex 88, 93
Senior Class Picnic 9, 82
Sheldon, Henry 27
Shelly, May Josephine 100
Shilts, Randy 103
Sigma Chi 48, 64, 65
Sigma Delta Chi, 49
Sigma Nu 24, 26, 42
Simeon, Dr. E. Joseph 12
Skip Day 17
Smith, Bev 90
Smith, Chloethiel Woodard 101
Smith, Ken 102

Spencer View 86
Stahl, Frank 92
Straub Hall 36
Straub, John 41
Streisinger, George 92
Streisinger Hall 86, 92
Strong, C.C. 12
Strong, Frank 14, 17, 19, 27
Student Army Training Corps 34
Student Health Facility 72
Student Recreation Center 86
Student Tennis Center 86
Student Union 38
Students for a Democratic Society 72
Students for a Progressive Agenda 86, 89

T
Tall Firs 44, 52
Theta Chi 72
Tomseth, Victor 102
Trine, O.W. "Dad" 18

U
University Day 20, 25, 82
University Inn 86

V
Villard Hall 13, 14, 17, 19, 20, 57, 66
Villard, Henry 14

W
Wallace, Lila Acheson 74
Walton Complex 72
Waring, Fred 60
Warner, Murray 30
Webfoot 42
Webfoots 39, 52, 105
Wei, Yung 102

Westmoreland Housing 72
Whiskerino 63, 69
Wickham, Golda 66, 77
Wiedemann, Kent 102
Wieden, Dan 103
Willamette Block 86
Willamette Hall 86
Willcox Building 69
Willoughby, Ruth 73
Wilson, O. Meredith 67, 70
Worker Rights Consortium 94
World War I 35
World War II 54, 55, 56

Y
YMCA 15
Young Americans for Freedom 72
YWCA 15

Z
Zebrafish Stock Center 86
Zorn-Macpherson Bill 46, 47, 60

Sources and Acknowledgments

Special thanks to Keith Richard, Barbara Edwards West, Tom Hager, Jessica MacMurray, James Fox, Heather Briston and Sharla Davis for their support and assistance in compiling this material.

Thanks also to the Office of the President and University Bookstore for their encouragement to create this history for our alumni, students and friends.

All photographs, with the exception of those listed below, courtesy of the University of Oregon Special Collections and Archives, University Photograph Collection.

Additional photo credits: University of Oregon Publications Office/Jack Liu: p. 89 top, p. 92 right, p. 93 bottom, p. 95, p. 97, p. 105. University of Oregon Publications Office: p. 102, p. 104 bottom left and bottom right. University of Oregon Athletics: p. 89 bottom. University of Oregon School of Law: p. 75.

Many of the articles appearing here were adapted from work originally printed in *Old Oregon/Oregon Quarterly*. Originals may be found in the UO Library. The first chapter, "The School on the Hill," was originally titled "Tough: Those First 25 Years."

OTHER SOURCES:
Mitchell, Sally. 1941. *The Life Story of Colonel William Hayward*. University of Oregon, student paper.
Oregon Daily Emerald. Various Years.
Oregana. Various Years.
Sheldon, Henry D. 1940. *History of the University of Oregon*. Portland: Binfords and Mort.
Shellenbarger, Michael, ed. 1989. *Harmony in Diversity: The Architecture and Teaching of Ellis F. Lawrence*. Eugene: School of Architecture and Allied Arts, University of Oregon.